Journey
of the
Cross

A PRAYER GUIDE FOR THE SEASON OF LENT
THROUGH THE GOSPEL OF JOHN

GRAHAM & SUSAN MICHAEL

College&Clayton Press

ATHENS, GEORGIA

College&Clayton
Press

Journey of the Cross: A Prayer Guide for the Season of Lent Through the Gospel of John
Copyright © 2023 Graham J. L. Michael

All rights reserved. No part of this publication may be used or reproduced in any manner whatsoever without written permission unless such quotation is covered by fair use. For information, contact College and Clayton Press, LLC., PO Box 5533, Athens, GA 30604.

College and Clayton Press website: https://collegeandclayton.com

Scripture quotations marked ESV have been taken from The *ESV® Bible (The Holy Bible, English Standard Version®)*, Copyright ©2001 by Crossway, a publishing ministry of Good News Publishers. Used by permission. All rights reserved.

Selections from the *Book of Common Prayer* are referenced with (BCP, *page #*). These selections are taken from *The Book of Common Prayer* (Church Publishing, Inc. 1979).

Cover and Interior Design: Daniel Blake Hulsey

ISBN: 978-1-956553-16-1

Printed in the United States of America

Contents:

Preface 1
The Journey of the Cross 3
How to Use this Guide 5
The Daily Practices 6
Fasting and Feasting.. 8

Ash Wednesday..12

Lent Week I: I AM the Bread of Life............................. 22

Lent Week II: I AM the Light of the World 38

Lent Week III: I AM the Door of the Sheep................ 54

Lent Week IV: I AM the Good Shepherd 70

Lent Week V: I AM the Way, the Truth, and the Life 86

Holy Week: I AM the Vine 102

Palm Sunday... 104
Maundy Thursday 112
Good Friday 114
Holy Saturday 116

Resurrection Sunday: I AM the Resurrection and the Life . 118

Appendix 1: 125
Finding our Place in the Story of the Gospel..........................125
Appendix II: 127
Praying the Lord's Prayer 127
Appendix III:...130
The Practice of Lectio Divina 130

Truly, truly, I say to you, unless a grain of wheat falls into the earth and dies, it remains alone; but if it dies, it bears much fruit. Whoever loves his life loses it, and whoever hates his life in this world will keep it for eternal life. If anyone serves me, he must follow me; and where I am, there will my servant be also. If anyone serves me, the Father will honor him.

John 12:24-26

Preface

For centuries, the church has intentionally and collectively engaged the season of Lent which culminates with the celebration of Easter. Together they prayed, studied, fasted, and feasted, all with the aim to prepare their hearts to celebrate once again the resurrection of Jesus Christ. Easter stands each year to remind us that we are part of a story that is greater than any one of us. A story that provides a hope and a future. A story that binds a people together under the banner of the Suffering Servant who became the victorious Resurrected King of all.

Although Easter is the day on which we celebrate the resurrection of Jesus Christ, it is not meant to be a celebration that is to come upon us suddenly, without notice, without preparation, without reflection. It is the culmination of a season, around which we are to alter, orient, and tune our lives. The aim of the season of Lent is to renew our focus and refresh our love for the Savior, by putting off the tangible comforts of the world in order to reflect upon the glorious nature of the cross. By embracing this journey of the cross—aligning the rhythms of our life with the life, death, and resurrection of Jesus Christ—we may put into practice the alignment of our story with his.

Therefore, Easter is more than a day. It is a season that is set aside and ordered according to the story of redemption, into which we are invited to enter through the cruciform life that bears witness that we belong to a Kingdom not of this world. Just as Jesus "sets his face to Jerusalem" (Luke 9:51) to suffer and die for the world, we are to follow him in this journey by denying ourselves, taking up our own cross, and following after Him (Luke 9:23). And being so united with him in his death, we are so united with him in his resurrection (Romans 6:5). As we thus embrace this season of fasting and repentance in light of the cross, we also prepare our hearts for feasting and celebration in light of His resurrection and the resurrection to come.

We pray that this guide may assist you in the journey of the cross during this season of Lent as you prepare your heart to celebrate the resurrection of Jesus Christ.

The Journey of the Cross

At the heart of the Christian faith is the cross of Jesus Christ, for it is greatest act and demonstration of God's love, by which we are brought into loving relationship with the Triune God. Yet, the life of Jesus was not merely a journey to the cross, for that was not the end—it was a journey of the cross, whose end was the resurrection, in which he was raised again to new life, bringing forth the beginning of a new creation.

By God's gracious design, the full story of the Gospel—the life, death, and resurrection of Jesus—is the story that is offered to each and every one of us. We are thus called into this journey of the cross, whose end is the resurrected life, the abundant life, in Jesus. It is in light of this journey of the cross, that we prepare our hearts to celebrate the glory of the resurrection.

What is the Season of Lent?

The "Church Calendar" was set up by the early church fathers who ordered time according to the story of Jesus Christ, which begins with Advent, followed by the season of Christmas to remember the incarnation and culminates with Easter to remember the crucifixion and resurrection. Lent is the season leading up to Easter, in which the Church prepares for the celebration of Jesus' atoning sacrifice for the sins of the world and his victory over death in his resurrection.

The season of Lent has been traditionally marked by the forty days leading up to Easter, beginning with the first day, which is "Ash Wednesday." The word Lent is from the Old English, "to lengthen," referring to the period of Spring when the days became longer. The significance of the number forty is associated with the period of temptation Jesus experiences in the wilderness as he fasted forty days and forty nights (Matthew 4; Luke 4), which not only served as the affirmation of his identity and role as the Son of God, but also the preparation for his ministry as the Messiah.

The Church has traditionally observed Lent by fasting, either from food and drink or some form of comfort or entertainment. Fasting takes place Monday through Saturday, making Sunday a day to feast, to enjoy and reflect on the thing from which you are fasting the rest of the week.

How to Use this Guide

This guide is designed in the long tradition of the Church observing the Season of Lent to experience God in Prayer, in Scripture, and in Reflection. Although the guide can be used as a personal devotion, this guide will be most effective if done with a community group or with a friend. The prayer for the Church is to participate in this journey of the cross together as a unified body, with hearts engaging the same rhythms and readings, praying the same prayers, reflecting on the same questions, all with the aim of being conformed more and more each day into the image of the Jesus.

Each day of the guide provides a form of worship with Daily Practices to shape the disposition of our heart, to set rhythms of worship for our soul, and to reflect upon the cross and resurrection of our Lord Jesus Christ. The aim is to approach the throne of God as his beloved child belonging to his holy people—established by Grace, formed by his Word, and sanctified by his Spirit—for our good and for his glory.

The guide will walk through the weeks of Lent beginning with Ash Wednesday and culminating with the final days of Easter: Maundy Thursday, Good Friday, Holy Saturday, and Resurrection Sunday. Each Sunday will focus on one of the seven I AM Statements from the Gospel of John with a reading from Isaiah that corresponds to the theme for that week. Monday through Saturday provides a short passage of the Gospel of John which will be completed in its entirety by the end of the Lent.

Please use this guide daily as you are able, in whole or in part. Let Scripture and prayer guide your thoughts, form your affections, and strengthen your peace. The following will look more in depth at the Daily Practices and the practices of Feasting and Fasting.

The Daily Practices

The prayer, intention, and hope for this guide is to help each person to experience the fullness of God more regularly and more deeply. The following framework describes each of the practices that are intended to provide pathways of grace through which to fellowship with the Lord, but may serve as a template, to be used as closely or as loosely as one may find helpful.

Silence and Stillness

Each morning will begin by practicing Silence and Stillness. This is an essential practice that helps us to order the scattered attention and affections of our hearts to be fully present with God. It is to help us to be still and know that he is God (Ps. 46:10).

Invitation to Meet with God

A passage from Scripture will invite us to meet with God. Out of the silence God speaks his Word, warmly inviting us to behold his grace, goodness, and glory.

Time of Confession

As we reflect on Christ's work on the cross to pay for our sin, we take time to search our hearts, confess the sin we continue to struggle with day by day, and thank God for his gracious promise to forgive us and cleanse us (1 John 1:6–9). Each day will provide a prayer to guide this time of confession.

Scripture Reading and Reflection

Every day we will be invited to read, to pray, and to live God's Word. We will read through the Gospel of John in its entirety over the course of Lent throughout the week, and on Sundays we will read a passage from Isaiah that is thematically related to the I AM statement for that week. The reflection questions are intended to help one to experience God in the contemplation of his Word to us. See the Appendix III for the ancient practice of prayerful reading of Scripture (Lectio Divina) for a deeper, slower, fuller engagement of each text.

Prayer of Adoration

After reading and reflecting on Scripture, we will take a moment to adore Jesus using language from the Lord's Prayer to form our prayers. See Appendix II for praying through the Lord's Prayer.

Commission to Serve the Lord

Each day will end with God's blessing and commission from his Word to live out the true story of the Gospel for the glory of the Triune God. Just as God's Word speaks first inviting us into fellowship with him, the Word speaks last to bless us to reflect his glory throughout our day.

Fasting and Feasting

Inasmuch as the story of the Gospel is formed by both the cross and the resurrection, the Season of Lent is marked by the rhythm of fasting and feasting. Fasting brings to focus the significance of the cross, while feasting anticipates the celebration of the resurrection.

Fasting

The season of Lent provides an opportunity to practice self-denial through fasting and repentance, enabling our hearts, souls, and minds to reflect upon and be formed by the weight of the cross.

Throughout the days of the week (Monday through Saturday), you are encouraged to engage in some type fasting, which is voluntarily going without food, or some other good or comfort regularly enjoyed. There are different types of fasting that one may partake during this time. The most common is a fast from food and drink, whether that is fasting from certain types of food or drink (such as dessert, caffeinated drinks, etc.), or fasting from all food on particular days (though, one should not fast from water). Other types could include fasting from entertainment such as TV, movies, music, the internet, or social media. The purpose of these fasts is to set aside the things that may ultimately distract us from self-reflection and communing with God.

It is important to note that fasting is not to be understood as a means by which we are able to get something from God or to earn his favor. Nor are we to fast so that we may be praised by others: as Jesus warns his followers not to partake in fasting and prayer in order to be seen by others (Matthew 6:16), we should be all the more careful not to bring attention to our disciplines, especially with posting on social media. Let your disposition and discipline be that your fasting "may not be seen by others but by your Father who is in secret. And your Father who sees in secret will reward you" (Matthew 6:18).

Fasting and prayer are to provide reflection upon the state of our souls in order that we may express our dependence upon God's provision, our desperation for God's grace, and our devotion to God's glory. In this way, fasting is not to be a burden of guilt but an opportunity for grace. In fact, we should understand our call to fast in light of our call to feast, in which our fasting from the things of this world anticipates our feasting with the King in his glory (Revelation 19:6–9).

Feasting

The season of Lent also provides an opportunity to practice celebration through feasting and fellowship, enabling our hearts, souls, and minds to anticipate and be formed by the glory of the resurrection.

Every Sunday, you are encouraged to engage in feasting. The feast can be the enjoyment of the thing from which you have decided to fast (such as desserts or caffeine), or it can simply be the enjoyment of a meal that intentionally focuses on God's grace, goodness, and glory. Since the Christian life is never meant to be lived in isolation the purpose of this guide is to be done together as the Body of Christ. Therefore, the feasts that we choose to observe should be intentional in gathering with our friends, family, and neighbors. The purpose of these feasts is to incline our hearts and our hopes to the glory of the resurrection to come.

Please take some time to pray and reflect upon the areas of your life where fasting might help you rely on the grace of God in order that you may better reflect on the glory of God. Also consider how you may spend your times of feasting with your family, friends, and neighbors to edify one another.

By His Grace for His Glory

As a final word of encouragement, this guide is in no way to be used as a measure for our righteousness nor should it become a burden for our guilt. Rather, it is meant to assist each of us to fix our eyes on Jesus Christ and encourage one another in this race of endurance (Hebrews 12:1–2). In this light, we should approach this guide with the grace that is found in Christ Jesus—for our good and for his glory.

O Lord, who hast mercy upon all,
take away from me my sins,
and mercifully kindle in me
the fire of thy Holy Spirit.
Take away from me the heart of stone,
and give me a heart of flesh,
a heart to love and adore Thee,
a heart to delight in Thee,
to follow and enjoy Thee,
for Christ's sake, Amen.

St. Ambrose of Milan (AD 339-397)

Ash Wednesday

Almighty and everlasting God, you hate nothing you have made, and you forgive the sins of all who are penitent: Create and make in us new and contrite hearts, that we, worthily lamenting our sins and acknowledging our wretchedness, may obtain of you, the God of all mercy, perfect remission and forgiveness; through Jesus Christ our Lord, who lives and reigns with you and the Holy Spirit, one God, for ever and ever.

Book of Common Prayer

Every year the Season of Lent begins with Ash Wednesday. In Scripture, ash or dust symbolizes death and frailty (Gen. 18:27), judgment (Deut. 28:24), mourning (Job 2:12), and repentance (Jonah 3:6). In this light, Ash Wednesday is meant for us to meditate on our own sin and death; that we come to terms that we are dust and to dust we shall return (Gen. 3:19).

As the Season of Lent is to prepare our hearts to celebrate the Resurrection of Jesus Christ on Easter, an important part of our preparation is to remember why Jesus Christ had to die in the first place. In the beginning, the first man and the first woman disobeyed God in the garden, desiring to live on their own terms instead of entrusting themselves to God's good will (Gen. 3). This rejection of God, who is our life and the length of our days, meant for them and for all humanity, death. In God's punishment for humanity's sin, He declares, "for you are dust, and to dust you shall return" (Gen. 3:19). Like Adam and Eve, we have all "gone astray; we have turned—every one—to his own way," and for this rebellion, "the LORD has laid on him the iniquity of us all" (Is. 53:6).

Ash Wednesday is thus meant to be a solemn reflection upon the profound truths of the Gospel, in which we are to:

1. Reflect upon our mortality, sinfulness, and need for the Savior
2. Repent of our sin and refocus our heart to follow Christ
3. Remember with confidence and gratitude that God has taken on our human nature to forgive us our sin, conquer death, and heal the world.[1]

Ash Wednesday
"For you are dust, and to dust you shall return"

Silence and Stillness
Take two whole minutes of complete silence and stillness to prepare your heart, soul, and mind to meet with the Lord. Be attentive to his love and care for you.

Invitation to Meet with God:
Psalm 119:25
My soul clings to the dust; give me life according to your Word!

Prayer for Ash Wednesday
Almighty and everlasting God, you hate nothing you have made, and you forgive the sins of all who are penitent: Create and make in us new and contrite hearts, that we, worthily lamenting our sins and acknowledging our wretchedness, may obtain of you, the God of all mercy, perfect remission and forgiveness; through Jesus Christ our Lord, who lives and reigns with you and the Holy Spirit, one God, for ever and ever (BCP, 217).

Scripture Reading and Reflection:
Genesis 3; John 1:1–5
1. Behold God: What does today's reading tell us about the Lord?
2. Live for God: How should we respond to the Word today?

Prayer of Adoration
Jesus, we acknowledge that there is a reason we had to be redeemed. All that touches our hands falls apart eventually. Left to ourselves, we, like the laws of entropy that govern our world, will fall into more disarray, not less. We confess we cannot save ourselves from the mess that we have made. We cannot make it all better. But thank you that we do not have to, for in your mercy you entered the muck and mire of our own making, and you took it on yourself and then gave us your goodness and righteousness and holiness instead. In the name of the Father, the Son, and the Holy Spirit, Amen.

Commission to Serve the Lord:
1 Corinthians 15:48–49

As was the man of dust, so also are those who are of the dust, and as is the man of heaven, so also are those who are of heaven. Just as we have borne the image of the man of dust, we shall also bear the image of the man of heaven.

Confess to God the Father: Confess your sins to the Lord, knowing that he is faithful and just to forgive us our sins and cleanse us from all unrighteousness (1 John 1:9)

Behold God in his Word: What does today's reading tell you about the Lord?

Live for God by his Spirit: How should you respond to God's word today?

Thursday
"For you are dust, and to dust you shall return"

Silence and Stillness
Take two whole minutes of complete silence and stillness to prepare your heart, soul, and mind to meet with the Lord. Be attentive to his love and care for you.

Invitation to Meet with God:
Psalm 103:13–14
As a father shows compassion to his children, so the LORD shows compassion to those who fear him. For he knows our frame; he remembers that we are dust.

Prayer of Confession
Most merciful God, whose goodness and steadfast love abounds to all whom you have created and redeemed, we confess that we have sinned against you and have fallen short of your glory. In your immeasurable grace, forgive us all our sins and cleanse us from all unrighteousness, that we may fear you and follow you all our days to the glory of your holy name. In the name of Father, the Son, and the Holy Spirit, we pray, Amen.

Scripture Reading and Reflection:
John 1:6–28
1. Behold Jesus: What does today's reading tell us about Jesus?
2. Live for Jesus: How should we respond to the Word today?

Prayer of Adoration
We acknowledge that the great exchange of our sin for your righteousness is the most critical we can ever make, and we make it gladly—Jesus in our place. Thank you that it's enough. That as we confess our sins you are faithful and just to forgive us and cleanse us from all unrighteousness (I Jn. 1:9). That there is now no condemnation for those who have hidden themselves in your goodness (Rom. 8:1). The work that you did on the cross has covered the sin and shame and given us a new life here and now and the hope of heaven in your presence for all eternity. In the name of the Father, the Son, and the Holy Spirit, Amen.

COMMISSION TO SERVE THE LORD:
HEBREWS 12:1

Therefore, since we are surrounded by so great a cloud of witnesses, let us also lay aside every weight, and sin which clings so closely, and let us run with endurance the race that is set before us.

Confess to God the Father: Confess your sins to the Lord, knowing that he is faithful and just to forgive us our sins and cleanse us from all unrighteousness (1 John 1:9)

_____
_____
_____
_____
_____
_____
_____
_____
_____

Behold God in his Word: What does today's reading tell you about the Lord?

_____
_____
_____
_____
_____
_____
_____
_____
_____

Live for God by his Spirit: How should you respond to God's word today?

_____
_____
_____
_____
_____
_____
_____
_____
_____

Friday
"For you are dust, and to dust you shall return"

Silence and Stillness
Take two whole minutes of complete silence and stillness to prepare your heart, soul, and mind to meet with the Lord. Be attentive to his love and care for you.

Invitation to Meet with God:
Psalm 109:21–22
But you, O GOD my Lord, deal on my behalf for your name's sake; because your steadfast love is good, deliver me! For I am poor and needy, and my heart is stricken within me.

Prayer of Confession
Gracious Lord, you are great and greatly to be praised for you alone are good and do good; we confess all the idols of our hearts that we have foolishly and feverishly made. They have distorted our souls, darkened our understanding, and destroyed our joy. In your greatness and goodness, demolish all the idols of our hearts, so that we may rightly glorify you and enjoy you alone, the one true God. In the name of Father, the Son, and the Holy Spirit, we pray, Amen.

Scripture Reading and Reflection:
John 1:29–51
1. Behold Jesus: What does today's reading tell us about Jesus?
2. Live for Jesus: How should we respond to the Word today?

Prayer of Adoration
We confess we have all sorts of ideas of how to serve you most effectively, Lord. We confess we, like Adam and Eve from the very beginning, think we know best how this whole thing works. Yet you, from the first have shown us an upside kingdom. Leading by serving. Laying down your life to save. We don't have the right instincts and we're sorry. Order and reorder our loves and allegiances and

methods until they look like yours. May we humble ourselves to serve and to love, just as you showed us. For as you said, no servant is greater than his master and we certainly are no exception. Less of us and more of you. In the name of the Father, the Son, and the Holy Spirit, Amen.

Commission to Serve the Lord: Ephesians 3:16

According to the riches of his glory may God grant you to be strengthened with power through his Spirit in your inner being, so that Christ may dwell in your hearts through faith.

Confess to God the Father: Confess your sins to the Lord, knowing that he is faithful and just to forgive us our sins and cleanse us from all unrighteousness (1 John 1:9)

_____
_____
_____
_____
_____
_____

Behold God in his Word: What does today's reading tell you about the Lord?

_____
_____
_____
_____
_____
_____
_____

Live for God by his Spirit: How should you respond to God's word today?

_____
_____
_____
_____
_____
_____
_____

Saturday
"For you are dust, and to dust you shall return"

Silence and Stillness
Take two whole minutes of complete silence and stillness to prepare your heart, soul, and mind to meet with the Lord. Be attentive to his love and care for you.

Invitation to Meet with God:
Psalm 113:5–7
Who is like the LORD our God, who is seated on high, who looks far down on the heavens and the earth? He raises the poor from the dust and lifts the needy from the ash heap.

Prayer of Confession
Almighty God, you love all things into existence and redeem all things into your love; we confess that our hearts have grown cold to the reality of your abundant love, unduly occupied with the empty nothings that steal away our attention, awareness, and affections. Renew in us a due sense of your loving presence, so that we may present our whole selves to you in love. In the name of Father, the Son, and the Holy Spirit, we pray, Amen.

Scripture Reading and Reflection:
John 2:1–25
1. Behold Jesus: What does today's reading tell us about Jesus?
2. Live for Jesus: How should we respond to the Word today?

Prayer of Adoration
Father, forgive us for holding the sacrifice of your Son so lightly, for scorning it to do what we want. Forgive us for doubting that a life surrendered to the one who loves us most and best will not be enough to satisfy. Since you did not spare even your own Son for us but gave him up for us all, won't you also surely give us everything else? (Romans 8:32). Thank you, thank you, Lord Jesus—for taking the pain and shame and death that we rightly deserved, and giving us abundant life and meaning in this world and

hope for the next in return. Thank you for being our deliverer, once and for all. In the name of the Father, the Son, and the Holy Spirit, Amen.

Commission to Serve the Lord:
Colossians 1:10–12

Walk in a manner worthy of the Lord, fully pleasing to him, bearing fruit in every good work and increasing in the knowledge of God; being strengthened with all power, according to his glorious might, for all endurance and patience with joy; giving thanks to the Father, who has qualified you to share in the inheritance of the saints in light.

Confess to God the Father: Confess your sins to the Lord, knowing that he is faithful and just to forgive us our sins and cleanse us from all unrighteousness (1 John 1:9)

_____
_____
_____
_____
_____
_____

Behold God in his Word: What does today's reading tell you about the Lord?

_____
_____
_____
_____
_____

Live for God by his Spirit: How should you respond to God's word today?

_____
_____
_____
_____
_____
_____
_____

First Sunday of Lent

Almighty God, whose blessed Son was led by the Spirit to be tempted by Satan: Come quickly to help us who are assaulted by many temptations; and, as you know the weaknesses of each of us, let each one find you mighty to save; through Jesus Christ your Son our Lord, who lives and reigns with you and the Holy Spirit, one God, now and for ever. Amen.

Book of Common Prayer

I AM THE BREAD OF LIFE
JOHN 6:35

In John 6:35, Jesus says, "I am the bread of life; whoever comes to me shall not hunger, and whoever believes in me shall never thirst." This is the response to the people's request to be given "the true bread from heaven" (6:33). But what they were seeking was not Jesus, but what Jesus had to offer. Jesus had just miraculously fed over 5,000 men (not counting women and children), with only five loaves and two fish (6:1–14). Having been satisfied with eating their fill of the loaves, they failed to read the signpost of this miracle: Jesus Christ is the manna, the true bread coming down from heaven that satisfies the soul and gives life to the world.

We are also faced with this temptation to seek Christ for what he can offer us instead of seeking Christ for himself. Christianity in our context today is too often presented as a means to gain position, power, and prosperity in this world. Yet, throughout the Gospels, Jesus never tries convincing people to follow him with empty promises that by doing so they will prosper financially, politically, or otherwise. In fact, he is unabashedly clear that to follow him would mean self-denial, taking up the cross, and suffering in this world (Luke 9:23; John 16:33). But even so, what the Father offers is himself by sending his Beloved Son to be received in the Holy Spirit. Jesus Christ is the true bread from heaven that gives life for eternity and empowers the abundant life today (John 10:10).

During the Season of Lent, the practice of fasting helps us to loosen our grip on the tangible comforts of the world that too easily and superficially satisfy our souls. We are made for so much more, to feed on Christ himself, to experience the real presence of the Triune God, to abide in him and he in us (John 6:53–56). May we seek Christ for himself, entrusting our lives to him, being fully satisfied in who he is.

First Sunday of Lent
"I AM the Bread of Life"

Silence and Stillness
Take two whole minutes of complete silence and stillness to prepare your heart, soul, and mind to meet with the Lord. Be attentive to his love and care for you.

Invitation to Meet with God:
Psalm 5:11
But let all who take refuge in you rejoice; let them ever sing for joy, and spread your protection over them, that those who love your name may exult in you.

Prayer for the First Sunday of Lent
Almighty God, whose blessed Son was led by the Spirit to be tempted by Satan: Come quickly to help us who are assaulted by many temptations; and, as you know the weaknesses of each of us, let each one find you mighty to save; through Jesus Christ your Son our Lord, who lives and reigns with you and the Holy Spirit, one God, now and for ever. Amen. (BCP, 218)

Scripture Reading and Reflection:
Isaiah 55
1. What does today's reading tell us about the LORD?
2. How should we respond to the Word today?

Prayer of Adoration
Jesus you are the one who knows what is in our hearts today. Only to you can we pour out our hearts before you, declaring that you are a refuge to us—because you already know exactly what actually has happened. And you are ready to hear us and you draw near to answer. We have questions, but we know that all the questions are answered fully and find their rest in you. So for now, we rest, and we wait and we trust that you are making all things new. In the name of the Father, the Son, and the Holy Spirit, Amen.

COMMISSION TO SERVE THE LORD:
PSALM 9:11

Sing praises to the LORD, who sits enthroned in Zion! Tell among the peoples his deeds!

Thank God the Father: "Give thanks always and for everything to God the Father in the name of our Lord Jesus Christ" (Eph. 5:20).

Behold God in his Word: What does today's reading tell you about the Lord?

Live for God by his Spirit: How should you respond to God's word today?

Monday | Lent I
"I AM the Bread of Life"

Silence and Stillness

Take two whole minutes of complete silence and stillness to prepare your heart, soul, and mind to meet with the Lord. Be attentive to his love and care for you.

Invitation to Meet with God:
Psalm 90:14

Satisfy us in the morning with your steadfast love, that we may rejoice and be glad all our days.

Prayer of Confession

God, our Bread of Life, who provides for all that we need each and every day, we confess our lack of trust in your faithful provision, trusting in our own ingenuity, craftiness, and resources, but not in you. Out of your amazing grace, give us the eyes to see all that you have seen fit to supply for our every need, so that we may give you thanks in every circumstance. In the name of Father, the Son, and the Holy Spirit, we pray, Amen.

Scripture Reading and Reflection:
John 3:1–15
1. Behold Jesus: What does today's reading tell us about the LORD?
2. Live for Jesus: How should we respond to the Word today?

Prayer of Adoration

Who in Heaven can be compared to you, God? Who among the sons of the mighty can be likened to you, Lord? Truly, who in heaven do we have but you? And on earth who is your equal? In every single way that counts, you are not like us. You are complete when we are broken. You are constant while we are tossed about by the emotion and circumstance of this present moment. Thank you that you never change, and that in your case that's a very good thing. We love you. In the name of the Father, the Son, and the Holy Spirit, Amen.

Commission to Serve the Lord:
2 Corinthians 1:3–4

> Blessed be the God and Father of our Lord Jesus Christ, the Father of mercies and God of all comfort, who comforts us in all our affliction, so that we may be able to comfort those who are in any affliction, with the comfort with which we ourselves are comforted by God.

Confess to God the Father: Confess your sins to the Lord, knowing that he is faithful and just to forgive us our sins and cleanse us from all unrighteousness (1 John 1:9)

Behold God in his Word: What does today's reading tell you about the Lord?

Live for God by his Spirit: How should you respond to God's word today?

Tuesday | Lent I
"I AM the Bread of Life"

Silence and Stillness
Take two whole minutes of complete silence and stillness to prepare your heart, soul, and mind to meet with the Lord. Be attentive to his love and care for you.

Invitation to Meet with God:
Psalm 107:8–9
Let them thank the LORD for his steadfast love, for his wondrous works to the children of man! For he satisfies the longing soul, and the hungry soul he fills with good things.

Prayer of Confession
King of Glory, who satisfies the deepest longings of our souls, we confess our disordered desires that fragment our affections and allegiance to you. In your overflowing generosity, fill our souls with all your fullness, unite our hearts to fear your name, and renew our minds, so that we may be wholly devoted to you. In the name of Father, the Son, and the Holy Spirit, we pray, Amen.

Scripture Reading and Reflection:
John 3:16–36
1. Behold Jesus: What does today's reading tell us about Jesus?
2. Live for Jesus: How should we respond to the Word today?

Prayer of Adoration
Lord, we fight for our own kingdoms with a fervor that never seems unquenchable and unending. Our kingdom. Our will. But you show us a better way. You trade our sad, failing kingdoms for your own. Our wills traded in for the wise rulings of a King whose ways are above our ways and whose thoughts are better than our thoughts. Your kingdom will stand, ours has already fallen. We submit with joy to your leading in our lives today. In the name of the Father, the Son, and the Holy Spirit, Amen.

Commission to Serve the Lord:
2 Corinthians 13:11

Finally, brothers and sisters, rejoice. Aim for restoration, comfort one another, agree with one another, live in peace; and the God of love and peace will be with you.

Confess to God the Father: Confess your sins to the Lord, knowing that he is faithful and just to forgive us our sins and cleanse us from all unrighteousness (1 John 1:9)

_____
_____
_____
_____
_____
_____
_____
_____

Behold God in his Word: What does today's reading tell you about the Lord?

_____
_____
_____
_____
_____
_____
_____
_____
_____

Live for God by his Spirit: How should you respond to God's word today?

_____
_____
_____
_____
_____
_____
_____
_____
_____

Wednesday | Lent I
"I AM the Bread of Life"

Silence and Stillness
Take two whole minutes of complete silence and stillness to prepare your heart, soul, and mind to meet with the Lord. Be attentive to his love and care for you.

Invitation to Meet with God:
Psalm 145:14–16
The LORD upholds all who are falling and raises up all who are bowed down. The eyes of all look to you, and you give them their food in due season. You open your hand; you satisfy the desire of every living thing.

Prayer of Confession
Almighty God, who daily bears us up, we confess that we have built such foolish fragile structures for our self-sufficiency, producing in us pride but failing to sustain us in all our burdens. In your merciful wisdom, take away all our false supports, so that we may cling to you as you cling to us. In the name of Father, the Son, and the Holy Spirit, we pray, Amen.

Scripture Reading and Reflection:
John 4:1–26
1. Behold Jesus: What does today's reading tell us about Jesus?
2. Live for Jesus: How should we respond to the Word today?

Prayer of Adoration
Thank you, Jesus that you care about our daily bread. Thank you that over and over again in your Word you tell us to ask you for what we need. You are not a God who is unfamiliar with what it is to be human, or what it is to be in need of the physical things that sustain us. God you are good and you do good so we ask in your mercy to provide for us this week. In each and every way. These are strange days, but you are still the God who sees us and knows just what we need even before we ask. We trust you today. Thank you for giving us what we need. In the name of the Father, the Son, and the Holy Spirit, Amen.

COMMISSION TO SERVE THE LORD:
1 THESSALONIANS 5:14–16

And we urge you, brothers, admonish the idle, encourage the fainthearted, help the weak, be patient with them all. See that no one repays anyone evil for evil, but always seek to do good to one another and to everyone. Rejoice always.

Confess to God the Father: Confess your sins to the Lord, knowing that he is faithful and just to forgive us our sins and cleanse us from all unrighteousness (1 John 1:9)

Behold God in his Word: What does today's reading tell you about the Lord?

Live for God by his Spirit: How should you respond to God's word today?

Thursday | Lent I
"I AM the Bread of Life"

Silence and Stillness

Take two whole minutes of complete silence and stillness to prepare your heart, soul, and mind to meet with the Lord. Be attentive to his love and care for you.

Invitation to Meet with God:
Psalm 146:5–7

Blessed is he whose help is the God of Jacob, whose hope is in the LORD his God, who made heaven and earth, the sea, and all that is in them, who keeps faith forever; who executes justice for the oppressed, who gives food to the hungry.

Prayer of Confession

God of all grace, who nourishes us with your Word, we confess that we have forsaken you as our living water and we have hewed out cisterns for ourselves—broken cisterns that can hold no water. In your overcoming kindness, implant your Word deep within our hearts, so that we may not sin against you. In the name of Father, the Son, and the Holy Spirit, we pray, Amen.

Scripture Reading and Reflection:
John 4:27–45

1. Behold Jesus: What does today's reading tell us about Jesus?
2. Live for Jesus: How should we respond to the Word today?

Prayer of Adoration

We have sinned, Lord. We know that and you know that. So in your grace, have mercy on us, for we know that we cannot fix ourselves. Search us, O God, and know our heart. Try us and know our thoughts. And see if there be any grievous way in us, and lead us in the way everlasting. We pray this for ourselves and for all your people. We thank you, God, that you care enough about us to continue the work of changing our hearts, and conforming us into the image of your Son. In the name of the Father, the Son, and the Holy Spirit, Amen.

Commission to Serve the Lord:
2 Thessalonians 2:16–17

Now may our Lord Jesus Christ himself, and God our Father, who loved us and gave us eternal comfort and good hope through grace, comfort your hearts and establish them in every good work and word.

Confess to God the Father: Confess your sins to the Lord, knowing that he is faithful and just to forgive us our sins and cleanse us from all unrighteousness (1 John 1:9)

Behold God in his Word: What does today's reading tell you about the Lord?

Live for God by his Spirit: How should you respond to God's word today?

Friday | Lent I
"I AM the Bread of Life"

Silence and Stillness
Take two whole minutes of complete silence and stillness to prepare your heart, soul, and mind to meet with the Lord. Be attentive to his love and care for you.

Invitation to Meet with God:
Psalm 22:25–26
From you comes my praise in the great congregation; my vows I will perform before those who fear him. The afflicted shall eat and be satisfied; those who seek him shall praise the LORD! May your hearts live forever!

Prayer of Confession
Everlasting God, who has given us the flesh of your only begotten Son so that we may feed on him, we confess that we have sought you, not because we have seen signs, but because we ate our fill of perishable loaves. In your steadfast love, help us in our unbelief to believe into the One whom you sent, the Bread from Heaven, so that we may live abundantly and eternally in Christ Jesus, our Lord. In the name of Father, the Son, and the Holy Spirit, we pray, Amen.

Scripture Reading and Reflection:
John 4:46–54
1. Behold Jesus: What does today's reading tell us about Jesus?
2. Live for Jesus: How should we respond to the Word today?

Prayer of Adoration
The world is wrecked with sin. At each turn, there is a chance to fall into evil. But you already know that. Would you not only deliver us from the evil inside and around us, but also lead us away from temptation? We are failing in this. But you have already won the battle, Jesus. We need only place our hand into yours and follow. Show us your ways. Lead us in your truth. We will follow you with joy. In the name of the Father, the Son, and the Holy Spirit, Amen.

Commission to Serve the Lord:
Hebrews 4:15–16

For we do not have a high priest who is unable to sympathize with our weaknesses, but one who in every respect has been tempted as we are, yet without sin. Let us then with confidence draw near to the throne of grace, that we may receive mercy and find grace to help in time of need.

Confess to God the Father: Confess your sins to the Lord, knowing that he is faithful and just to forgive us our sins and cleanse us from all unrighteousness (1 John 1:9)

_____
_____
_____
_____
_____
_____
_____
_____
_____

Behold God in his Word: What does today's reading tell you about the Lord?

_____
_____
_____
_____
_____
_____
_____
_____
_____

Live for God by his Spirit: How should you respond to God's word today?

_____
_____
_____
_____
_____
_____
_____
_____
_____

Saturday | Lent I
"I AM the Bread of Life"

Silence and Stillness
Take two whole minutes of complete silence and stillness to prepare your heart, soul, and mind to meet with the Lord. Be attentive to his love and care for you.

Invitation to Meet with God:
Psalm 63:5–8
My soul will be satisfied as with fat and rich food, and my mouth will praise you with joyful lips, when I remember you upon my bed, and meditate on you in the watches of the night; for you have been my help, and in the shadow of your wings I will sing for joy. My soul clings to you; your right hand upholds me.

Prayer of Confession
Blessed Lord, who gladdens the hearts of your people with the truth, goodness, and beauty of your creation to reflect your glory and refresh our souls, we confess that we have in vain risen early and gone late to rest, eating the bread of anxious toil, for you give to your beloved sleep. In the gentleness of your heart, give rest to all those who labor and are heavy laden, so that we may take your yoke upon us, learn from you, and find rest for our souls. In the name of Father, the Son, and the Holy Spirit, we pray, Amen.

Scripture Reading and Reflection:
John 5:1–17
1. Behold Jesus: What does today's reading tell us about Jesus?
2. Live for Jesus: How should we respond to the Word today?

Prayer of Adoration
You promise that the sad and bad and hard of this world will one day be made perfectly whole. But that day is not today. While we wait, we ask that you still show us your kingdom, your power, your glory here on earth. Encourage our hearts as we walk roads that do not yet make sense to

us. Remind us that we are pilgrims here, our home is another Country. Lead us further in and further up, Lord. In the name of the Father, the Son, and the Holy Spirit, Amen.

Commission to Serve the Lord:
James 4:8–10

Draw near to God, and he will draw near to you. Cleanse your hands, you sinners, and purify your hearts, you double-minded. Be wretched and mourn and weep. Let your laughter be turned to mourning and your joy to gloom. Humble yourselves before the Lord, and he will exalt you.

Confess to God the Father: Confess your sins to the Lord, knowing that he is faithful and just to forgive us our sins and cleanse us from all unrighteousness (1 John 1:9)

Behold God in his Word: What does today's reading tell you about the Lord?

Live for God by his Spirit: How should you respond to God's word today?

Second Sunday of Lent

O God, whose glory it is always to have mercy: Be gracious to all who have gone astray from your ways, and bring them again with penitent hearts and steadfast faith to embrace and hold fast the unchangeable truth of your Word, Jesus Christ your Son; who with you and the Holy Spirit lives and reigns, one God, for ever and ever. Amen.

Book of Common Prayer

I AM THE LIGHT OF THE WORLD
JOHN 8:12

In John 7, Jesus attends the Feast of Tabernacles, which is a weeklong festival that is established in the Torah and was associated with the ingathering of the autumn harvest (Lev. 22:33–44; Num. 29:35–38; Deut. 16:13–17). Traditionally, towards the end of the festival, four huge lamps in the temple's court of women were lit, followed by an extraordinary celebration with lights illuminating all of Jerusalem. This celebration was most certainly an allusion to the coming of Yahweh in which the world will be flooded with everlasting light (cf. Zech. 14:7). It is within this context, that Jesus declares, "I am the light of the world. Whoever follows me will not walk in darkness, but will have the light of life" (8:12).[2]

With this statement, Jesus draws to himself all the vast and rich images of light used to describe the gracious activity of God: God's first act of creation bringing light out of the darkness (Gen. 1:4), God's cloud leading the people through the wilderness (Exod. 13:21–22), God's word illuminating the wise and faithful (Ps. 119:105), God's plan of cosmic redemption including the nations (Is. 49:6). As one scholar puts it: "Light is Yahweh in action."[3]

Jesus thus identifies with Yahweh, who is our light and our salvation (Ps. 27:1), and in whose light do we see light (Ps. 36:9). And as the light who is the light of all people (Jn. 1:4), Jesus has tabernacled among us (Jn. 1:14), inviting us to follow him, walking not in the darkness but in his light. Therefore, during this season of Lent, let us seek to behold his glory, that being so transformed, we may reflect his glory to the world (2 Cor. 3:18).

Second Sunday of Lent
"I Am the Light of the World"

Silence and Stillness
Take two whole minutes of complete silence and stillness to prepare your heart, soul, and mind to meet with the Lord. Be attentive to his love and care for you.

Call to Worship the Lord:
Psalm 10:16–18
The LORD is king forever and ever; the nations perish from his land. O LORD, you hear the desire of the afflicted; you will strengthen their heart; you will incline your ear to do justice to the fatherless and the oppressed, so that man who is of the earth may strike terror no more.

Prayer for the Second Sunday of Lent
O God, whose glory it is always to have mercy: Be gracious to all who have gone astray from your ways, and bring them again with penitent hearts and steadfast faith to embrace and hold fast the unchangeable truth of your Word, Jesus Christ your Son; who with you and the Holy Spirit lives and reigns, one God, for ever and ever. Amen (BCP, 218).

Scripture Reading and Reflection:
Isaiah 60
1. What does today's reading tell us about the LORD?
2. How should we respond to the Word today?

Prayer of Adoration
Jesus, this world can be very, very hard. And right now so many things are. We hear you when you tell us not to fear, that you have redeemed us and called us by name. When we pass through the waters you will be with us. So we will not be afraid, because you are with us. You are no stranger to our weakness and suffering. You see us and you know. We trust you. Show us what walking in your ways looks like, right here, right now, and we'll do it. In the name of the Father, the Son, and the Holy Spirit, Amen.

COMMISSION TO SERVE THE LORD:
PSALM 9:11
> Sing praises to the LORD, who sits enthroned in Zion! Tell among the peoples his deeds!

Thank God the Father: "Give thanks always and for everything to God the Father in the name of our Lord Jesus Christ" (Eph. 5:20).

Behold God in his Word: What does today's reading tell you about the Lord?

Live for God by his Spirit: How should you respond to God's word today?

Monday | Lent II
"I Am the Light of the World"

Silence and Stillness
Take two whole minutes of complete silence and stillness to prepare your heart, soul, and mind to meet with the Lord. Be attentive to his love and care for you.

Invitation to Meet with God:
Psalm 4:6
There are many who say, "Who will show us some good? Lift up the light of your face upon us, O LORD!" You have put more joy in my heart than they have when their grain and wine abound.

Prayer of Confession
God, the Light of the World, whose light shines in the darkness and the darkness has not overcome it, we confess all the ways we have taken part in the unfruitful works of darkness. By your glory and for your glory, expose the things now hidden in darkness, disclosing the purposes of our heart, that we may walk in the light as you are in the light. In the name of Father, the Son, and the Holy Spirit, we pray, Amen.

Scripture Reading and Reflection:
John 5:18–29
1. Behold Jesus: What does today's reading tell us about Jesus?
2. Live for Jesus: How should we respond to the Word today?

Prayer of Adoration
We are constrained by our humanness, and from our birth you can take our measure. What we are and what we are not. But not you. You have no measure and no limit to your power, to your holiness. Yet you chose to limit yourself to take on flesh with all its constraints and walk among us so you could say with confidence that you are not unfamiliar with the burdens we bear. Yet you still did it all without sin. Even as you became like us, you were still all that we could not be. Thank you Jesus for living a life that we could not live and dying the death that was meant for us. In the name of the Father, the Son, and the Holy Spirit, Amen.

COMMISSION TO SERVE THE LORD:
TITUS 3:1–2

> Be submissive to rulers and authorities, to be obedient, to be ready for every good work, to speak evil of no one, to avoid quarreling, to be gentle, and to show perfect courtesy toward all people.

Confess to God the Father: Confess your sins to the Lord, knowing that he is faithful and just to forgive us our sins and cleanse us from all unrighteousness (1 John 1:9)

_____
_____
_____
_____
_____
_____
_____
_____
_____

Behold God in his Word: What does today's reading tell you about the Lord?

_____
_____
_____
_____
_____
_____
_____
_____
_____

Live for God by his Spirit: How should you respond to God's word today?

_____
_____
_____
_____
_____
_____
_____
_____
_____

Tuesday | Lent II
"I Am the Light of the World"

Silence and Stillness
Take two whole minutes of complete silence and stillness to prepare your heart, soul, and mind to meet with the Lord. Be attentive to his love and care for you.

Invitation to Meet with God:
Psalm 18:28–30
For it is you who light my lamp; the LORD my God lightens my darkness. For by you I can run against a troop, and by my God I can leap over a wall. This God—his way is perfect; the word of the LORD proves true; he is a shield for all those who take refuge in him.

Prayer of Confession
King of Glory, who graciously reveals yourself in cloud and fire to guide your people through the wilderness, we confess all the torches we have kindled for ourselves, not trusting in the light you provide. Without you, Lord, we stumble in this present darkness. In your goodness, illuminate the eyes of our hearts that we may entrust ourselves completely to your most gracious will. In the name of Father, the Son, and the Holy Spirit, we pray, Amen.

Scripture Reading and Reflection:
John 5:30–47
1. Behold Jesus: What does today's reading tell us about Jesus?
2. Live for Jesus: How should we respond to the Word today?

Prayer of Adoration
Lord Jesus, your kingdom far outshines the weak attempts at empire building our hearts and minds have produced. Yet we continue to fight for our rights to build them. Forgive us. Forgive us for the rebellion in our hearts that continues to spread the lie that we can do this on our own. We acknowledge with joy that we cannot produce anything that matters apart from you. We need you every hour. Thank you for being all that we cannot be today. In the name of the Father, the Son, and the Holy Spirit, Amen.

COMMISSION TO SERVE THE LORD:
JAMES 3:17–18
> But the wisdom from above is first pure, then peaceable, gentle, open to reason, full of mercy and good fruits, impartial and sincere. And a harvest of righteousness is sown in peace by those who make peace.

Confess to God the Father: Confess your sins to the Lord, knowing that he is faithful and just to forgive us our sins and cleanse us from all unrighteousness (1 John 1:9)

_____
_____
_____
_____
_____
_____
_____
_____

Behold God in his Word: What does today's reading tell you about the Lord?

_____
_____
_____
_____
_____
_____
_____
_____

Live for God by his Spirit: How should you respond to God's word today?

_____
_____
_____
_____
_____
_____
_____
_____

Wednesday | Lent II
"I Am the Light of the World"

Silence and Stillness
Take two whole minutes of complete silence and stillness to prepare your heart, soul, and mind to meet with the Lord. Be attentive to his love and care for you.

Invitation to Meet with God:
Psalm 89:14–16
Righteousness and justice are the foundation of your throne; steadfast love and faithfulness go before you. Blessed are the people who know the festal shout, who walk, O LORD, in the light of your face, who exult in your name all the day and in your righteousness are exalted.

Prayer of Confession
Almighty God, whose Beloved Son is the true light that has come into the world, revealing your grace and truth, we confess that, although we were made through him and for him, our lives often reflect that we do not know him. As you have called us out of darkness into your marvelous light, may your Spirit empower us to walk as children of the light to the glory of your holy name. In the name of Father, the Son, and the Holy Spirit, we pray, Amen.

Scripture Reading and Reflection:
John 6:1–15
1. Behold Jesus: What does today's reading tell us about Jesus?
2. Live for Jesus: How should we respond to the Word today?

Prayer of Adoration
God, you have always provided for us in the past. Your faithfulness has been tested and found true at each turn. We are a faithless, forgetful people, but you are an utterly faithful, always remembering God who cares for us. Thank you that as you have always provided, you will continue to do so. We trust you for the needs of this day, Jesus. We thank you that you are even now providing all that is required. In the name of the Father, the Son, and the Holy Spirit, Amen.

Commission to Serve the Lord:
Galatians 5:22–24

But the fruit of the Spirit is love, joy, peace, patience, kindness, goodness, faithfulness, gentleness, self-control; against such things there is no law. And those who belong to Christ Jesus have crucified the flesh with its passions and desires.

Confess to God the Father: Confess your sins to the Lord, knowing that he is faithful and just to forgive us our sins and cleanse us from all unrighteousness (1 John 1:9)

_____
_____
_____
_____
_____
_____
_____
_____
_____

Behold God in his Word: What does today's reading tell you about the Lord?

_____
_____
_____
_____
_____
_____
_____
_____
_____

Live for God by his Spirit: How should you respond to God's word today?

_____
_____
_____
_____
_____
_____
_____
_____
_____

Thursday | Lent II
"I Am the Light of the World"

Silence and Stillness
Take two whole minutes of complete silence and stillness to prepare your heart, soul, and mind to meet with the Lord. Be attentive to his love and care for you.

Invitation to Meet with God:
Psalm 97:10
Light is sown for the righteous, and joy for the upright in heart. Rejoice in the LORD, O you righteous, and give thanks to his holy name!

Prayer of Confession
Gracious Redeemer, you have delivered us from the domain of darkness and transferred us to the kingdom of your Beloved Son. We confess all the times that we have remained in the shadows of complacency, neglecting the calling to which you have called us. As your church, empower us to fan into flame the gifts you have given us by your Spirit, awaking our glory, so that we may glorify your name in all the world. In the name of Father, the Son, and the Holy Spirit, we pray, Amen.

Scripture Reading and Reflection:
John 6:16–40
1. Behold Jesus: What does today's reading tell us about Jesus?
2. Live for Jesus: How should we respond to the Word today?

Prayer of Adoration
Jesus, you have made provision for our sin by your death on the cross. We know that because of your work and by the power of the Holy Spirit, you can and will cleanse us from all our sin and all of our bent ways and bring us closer to you. Thanks Jesus that it's your work and your goodness that can do this—not our own attempts at conjuring up goodness in ourselves. We ask your forgiveness for the things we have done and left undone. For the things we said without consideration of the name we now represent. We thank you for being faithful and just to forgive us our

sins and to cleanse us, Lord. In the name of the Father, the Son, and the Holy Spirit, Amen.

Commission to Serve the Lord: Romans 14:7–9

For none of us lives to himself, and none of us dies to himself. For if we live, we live to the Lord, and if we die, we die to the Lord. So then, whether we live or whether we die, we are the Lord's. For to this end Christ died and lived again, that he might be Lord both of the dead and of the living.

Confess to God the Father: Confess your sins to the Lord, knowing that he is faithful and just to forgive us our sins and cleanse us from all unrighteousness (1 John 1:9)

_____
_____
_____
_____
_____
_____

Behold God in his Word: What does today's reading tell you about the Lord?

_____
_____
_____
_____
_____
_____
_____

Live for God by his Spirit: How should you respond to God's word today?

_____
_____
_____
_____
_____
_____
_____
_____

Friday | Lent II
"I Am the Light of the World"

Silence and Stillness
Take two whole minutes of complete silence and stillness to prepare your heart, soul, and mind to meet with the Lord. Be attentive to his love and care for you.

Invitation to Meet with God:
Psalm 118:26–27
Blessed is he who comes in the name of the LORD! We bless you from the house of the LORD. The LORD is God, and he has made his light to shine upon us. Bind the festal sacrifice with cords, up to the horns of the altar!

Prayer of Confession
Everlasting God, with you is the fountain of life and in your light do we see light. We confess that we have closed our eyes to the injustices of the world, leaving us dark within and without. Since the night is far gone and the day is at hand, help us cast off the works of darkness and put on the armor of light, so that we may have fellowship with your light that brings healing and holiness to the world. In the name of Father, the Son, and the Holy Spirit, we pray, Amen.

Scripture Reading and Reflection:
John 6:41–59
1. Behold Jesus: What does today's reading tell us about Jesus?
2. Live for Jesus: How should we respond to the Word today?

Prayer of Adoration
Lord, we are unable to save ourselves. This has been proven without exception. On our own we will plummet further into the hole our own actions and the actions of others have dug for us. But that is not your way. When we were flailing about helpless, you saved us and put our feet on the rock. In your sovereignty, you provide us a way out and into flourishing. Thank you, Jesus, that you do not leave us to our own foolish devices. Thank you for saving us. In the name of the Father, the Son, and the Holy Spirit, Amen.

COMMISSION TO SERVE THE LORD:
2 CORINTHIANS 9:8
> And God is able to make all grace abound to you, so that having all sufficiency in all things at all times, you may abound in every good work.

Confess to God the Father: Confess your sins to the Lord, knowing that he is faithful and just to forgive us our sins and cleanse us from all unrighteousness (1 John 1:9)

_____
_____
_____
_____
_____
_____
_____
_____

Behold God in his Word: What does today's reading tell you about the Lord?

_____
_____
_____
_____
_____
_____
_____
_____

Live for God by his Spirit: How should you respond to God's word today?

_____
_____
_____
_____
_____
_____
_____
_____

Saturday | Lent II
"I Am the Light of the World"

Silence and Stillness
Take two whole minutes of complete silence and stillness to prepare your heart, soul, and mind to meet with the Lord. Be attentive to his love and care for you.

Invitation to Meet with God:
Psalm 139:11–12
If I say, "Surely the darkness shall cover me, and the light about me be night," even the darkness is not dark to you; the night is bright as the day, for darkness is as light with you.

Prayer of Confession
Blessed Lord, in your tender mercy, whereby the sunrise visits us from on high, you give light to those who sit in darkness. We confess our dull labor and our dim hearts that are in desperate need of the light of your Sabbath. Send out your light and your truth and let them lead us; let them bring us to your holy mountain and to your dwelling, that we may rest in your presence and peace. In the name of Father, the Son, and the Holy Spirit, we pray, Amen.

Scripture Reading and Reflection:
John 6:60–71
1. Behold Jesus: What does today's reading tell us about Jesus?
2. Live for Jesus: How should we respond to the Word today?

Prayer of Adoration
Lord, from the day of our birth we've been building our little domains and asserting our power to rule them. You know our hearts. You see the tendencies and the well beaten pathways towards crowing ourselves the rulers of whatever it is we're doing and building. We're sorry. We're wrong and we're sorry. Yours is the kingdom. Yours is the power. It is your right to build our lives according to your kingdom. You have bought us with the blood of your Son--you've called us your children and your heirs with Christ. We choose your kingdom and your power. In the name of the Father, the Son, and the Holy Spirit, Amen.

COMMISSION TO SERVE THE LORD:
2 CORINTHIANS 12:9–10

> But he said to me, "My grace is sufficient for you, for my power is made perfect in weakness." Therefore I will boast all the more gladly of my weaknesses, so that the power of Christ may rest upon me. For the sake of Christ, then, I am content with weaknesses, insults, hardships, persecutions, and calamities. For when I am weak, then I am strong.

Confess to God the Father: Confess your sins to the Lord, knowing that he is faithful and just to forgive us our sins and cleanse us from all unrighteousness (1 John 1:9)

Behold God in his Word: What does today's reading tell you about the Lord?

Live for God by his Spirit: How should you respond to God's word today?

Third Sunday of Lent

Almighty God, you know that we have no power in ourselves to help ourselves: Keep us both outwardly in our bodies and inwardly in our souls, that we may be defended from all adversities which may happen to the body, and from all evil thoughts which may assault and hurt the soul; through Jesus Christ our Lord, who lives and reigns with you and the Holy Spirit, one God, for ever and ever. Amen.

Book of Common Prayer

I AM the Door of the Sheep
John 10:7

In John 10, Jesus provides a matrix of metaphors that include shepherds, sheep, pastures, and bandits, all to convey that he is the sole means of salvation and flourishing. Jesus declares, "I am the Door of the Sheep" (10:7), which means he is the only way through which to have eternal Life and Life abundantly. Those who come before Jesus are called thieves and robbers. They are the counterfeit messiahs who promise prosperity, power, and prestige, but only bring about death, despair, and destruction. They are the ones who seek to achieve glory with their own ability according to their own appetites apart from the grace of God. The sheep do not listen to these voices but listen to the voice of the Shepherd who calls them by name and leads them into green pastures.

Jesus tells us that the thief comes to steal and kill and destroy (10:10). This thief may represent the devil or any worldly power that offers salvation and flourishing apart from Jesus Christ. This vision often excludes self-denial, being poured out for others, and suffering for the sake of righteousness. But this way only leads to disenchantment and despair. Jesus promises that he is the means of salvation (eternal life) and flourishing (abundant life). It is only through Jesus that we may receive salvation for our souls, to live eternally with the Father. It is only through Jesus that we may live meaningful lives in the face of a broken world in the midst of suffering.

More than ever today we are tempted to look for doors or paths or means by which to have abundant life, whether through politics, technology, or even religion. But Jesus always puts before us himself as our only entrance to the Life for which we were created and have always desired. Let us listen to the voice of the One calling us by name and enter the Door by which we enter Life itself and find rest for our souls.

Third Sunday of Lent
"I Am the Door of the Sheep."

Silence and Stillness
Take two whole minutes of complete silence and stillness to prepare your heart, soul, and mind to meet with the Lord. Be attentive to his love and care for you.

Invitation to Meet with God:
Psalm 17:15
As for me, I shall behold your face in righteousness; when I awake, I shall be satisfied with your likeness.

Prayer for the Third Sunday of Lent
Almighty God, you know that we have no power in ourselves to help ourselves: Keep us both outwardly in our bodies and inwardly in our souls, that we may be defended from all adversities which may happen to the body, and from all evil thoughts which may assault and hurt the soul; through Jesus Christ our Lord, who lives and reigns with you and the Holy Spirit, one God, for ever and ever. Amen (BCP, 218).

Scripture Reading and Reflection:
Isaiah 26:1–6
1. What does today's reading tell us about the LORD?
2. How should we respond to the Word today?

Prayer of Adoration
Lord you tell us that you are our portion, but we confess we struggle to believe it. We see scarcity all around us and inside us. Remind us, Provider, that you sustain us with a word when we are weary, giving strength and joy when we have nothing left. Convict us of where we are finding our peace and rest and sustenance, and reorient our hearts to look only to you. As Peter said, where else would we go? Only you have the words that bring of life. We trust that you are making ways for us. In the name of the Father, the Son, and the Holy Spirit, Amen.

Commission to Serve the Lord and his Kingdom: Psalm 47:5–7

God has gone up with a shout, the LORD with the sound of a trumpet. Sing praises to God, sing praises! Sing praises to our King, sing praises! For God is the King of all the earth; sing praises with a psalm!

Thank God the Father: "Give thanks always and for everything to God the Father in the name of our Lord Jesus Christ" (Eph. 5:20).

Behold God in his Word: What does today's reading tell you about the Lord?

Live for God by his Spirit: How should you respond to God's word today?

Monday | Lent III
"I Am the Door of the Sheep"

Silence and Stillness
Take two whole minutes of complete silence and stillness to prepare your heart, soul, and mind to meet with the Lord. Be attentive to his love and care for you.

Invitation to Meet with God:
Psalm 26:8
O LORD, I love the habitation of your house and the place where your glory dwells.

Prayer of Confession
God, the Door of the Sheep, through whom we find our salvation, security, and satisfaction, we confess that we have longed for pastures outside of your grace, making our hearts to wander in the wilderness of our futile works. In your compassion, settle our hearts solely in the land of your good pleasure, so that we may find our joy in you. In the name of Father, the Son, and the Holy Spirit, we pray, Amen.

Scripture Reading and Reflection:
John 7:1–24
1. Behold Jesus: What does today's reading tell us about Jesus?
2. Live for Jesus: How should we respond to the Word today?

Prayer of Adoration
Lord God, we thank you that you do not become less holy by taking on our lot—you just make everything around you holy as you go. And that includes us. You chose us to be in your family. Through you we may become children of God. You are conforming us into your image, all this to the praise of your glory, not ours. And you deserve every ounce of that glory, God. We give it to you with joy. In the name of the Father, the Son, and the Holy Spirit, Amen.

Commission to Serve the Lord and his Kingdom:
Romans 6:12–13
Let not sin therefore reign in your mortal body, to make you obey its passions. Do not present your members to sin as

instruments for unrighteousness, but present yourselves to God as those who have been brought from death to life, and your members to God as instruments for righteousness.

Confess to God the Father: Confess your sins to the Lord, knowing that he is faithful and just to forgive us our sins and cleanse us from all unrighteousness (1 John 1:9)

_____
_____
_____
_____
_____
_____
_____
_____

Behold God in his Word: What does today's reading tell you about the Lord?

_____
_____
_____
_____
_____
_____
_____
_____

Live for God by his Spirit: How should you respond to God's word today?

_____
_____
_____
_____
_____
_____
_____
_____
_____
_____

Tuesday | Lent III
"I Am the Door of the Sheep"

Silence and Stillness
Take two whole minutes of complete silence and stillness to prepare your heart, soul, and mind to meet with the Lord. Be attentive to his love and care for you.

Invitation to Meet with God:
Psalm 27:4
One thing have I asked of the LORD, that will I seek after: that I may dwell in the house of the LORD all the days of my life, to gaze upon the beauty of the LORD and to inquire in his temple.

Prayer of Confession
King of Glory, you have been our dwelling place in all generations; before the mountains were brought forth, or ever you had formed the earth and the world, from everlasting to everlasting, you are God. We confess that we have strayed away from you, looking and longing for that which will never satisfy our souls. Bring our hearts back to the fold of your grace, that we may enter more deeply into your steadfast love. In the name of Father, the Son, and the Holy Spirit, we pray, Amen.

Scripture Reading and Reflection:
John 7:25–39
1. Behold Jesus: What does today's reading tell us about Jesus?
2. Live for Jesus: How should we respond to the Word today?

Prayer of Adoration
Our Lord Jesus, our wills have made this world a disaster. Your kingdom come and may it come soon. We need what you have to offer us because the fixes and solutions we have to bind up this weary and broken world are not working. Our world needs a rest from its toil and labors that only kingdom with you as its rightful King can offer. So come, King Jesus. Fix what we've broken. We trust you to do this as only you can. In the name of the Father, the Son, and the Holy Spirit, Amen.

Commission to Serve the Lord and his Kingdom: Ephesians 5:15–18

> Look carefully then how you walk, not as unwise but as wise, making the best use of the time, because the days are evil. Therefore do not be foolish, but understand what the will of the Lord is. And do not get drunk with wine, for that is debauchery, but be filled with the Spirit.

Confess to God the Father: Confess your sins to the Lord, knowing that he is faithful and just to forgive us our sins and cleanse us from all unrighteousness (1 John 1:9)

_____
_____
_____
_____
_____
_____
_____

Behold God in his Word: What does today's reading tell you about the Lord?

_____
_____
_____
_____
_____
_____
_____
_____

Live for God by his Spirit: How should you respond to God's word today?

_____
_____
_____
_____
_____
_____
_____
_____
_____

Wednesday | Lent III
"I Am the Door of the Sheep"

Silence and Stillness
Take two whole minutes of complete silence and stillness to prepare your heart, soul, and mind to meet with the Lord. Be attentive to his love and care for you.

Invitation to Meet with God:
Psalm 52:8–9
But I am like a green olive tree in the house of God. I trust in the steadfast love of God forever and ever. I will thank you forever, because you have done it. I will wait for your name, for it is good, in the presence of the godly.

Prayer of Confession
Almighty God, you alone are our home and happiness, the sanctuary for our souls. We confess that our hearts have been entangled in the desires of this world, the deceitfulness of riches, and the despair of this age, which have choked your Word making us unfruitful for your Kingdom. Enrich the soil of our hearts for your Word to take deep root, so that our lives may bear fruitful witness for your name in all the world. In the name of Father, the Son, and the Holy Spirit, we pray, Amen.

Scripture Reading and Reflection:
John 7:40–52
1. Behold Jesus: What does today's reading tell us about Jesus?
2. Live for Jesus: How should we respond to the Word today?

Prayer of Adoration
We need your help, Jesus. Today we need your help as the world around us feels so broken. And the path set for our feet is more uncertain than ever. But you are the God who made us in our mothers' wombs. You knew us before we were born. And you see us and know us now. Our health is in your hands. The health of our families is in your hand. Thank you that we can place them back in your hands again today with confidence that you are good and you do good. We trust that you are providing what we need today.

In the name of the Father, the Son, and the Holy Spirit, Amen.

COMMISSION TO SERVE THE LORD AND HIS KINGDOM: PHILIPPIANS 1:9–11

May your abound more and more, with knowledge and all discernment, so that you may approve what is excellent, and so be pure and blameless for the day of Christ, filled with the fruit of righteousness that comes through Jesus Christ, to the glory and praise of God.

Confess to God the Father: Confess your sins to the Lord, knowing that he is faithful and just to forgive us our sins and cleanse us from all unrighteousness (1 John 1:9)

___

Behold God in his Word: What does today's reading tell you about the Lord?

___

Live for God by his Spirit: How should you respond to God's word today?

___

Thursday | Lent III
"I Am the Door of the Sheep"

Silence and Stillness
Take two whole minutes of complete silence and stillness to prepare your heart, soul, and mind to meet with the Lord. Be attentive to his love and care for you.

Invitation to Meet with God:
Psalm 65:4
Blessed is the one you choose and bring near, to dwell in your courts! We shall be satisfied with the goodness of your house, the holiness of your temple!

Prayer of Confession
God, our Redeemer, you have spoken in your Word and in your Word you still speak today. We confess that we have not listened to your voice calling to us, but with itching ears we have heaped up for ourselves voices that speak to our own passions, turning us away from your truth and making us wander off into falsehoods. Silence every voice that is not yours and give us ears to hear all that you have to tell us in your Word. In the name of Father, the Son, and the Holy Spirit, we pray, Amen.

Scripture Reading and Reflection:
John 8:1–30
1. Behold Jesus: What does today's reading tell us about Jesus?
2. Live for Jesus: How should we respond to the Word today?

Prayer of Adoration
We are not good at this, Lord. Any of it, if we're honest. We do what we should not do, and we don't do the things we should. Forgive us. Humble us to remember just how much there is in need of forgiveness in our lives. Thank you for being the Just and Good King who is faithful to forgive the dark and twisted places. Thank you that you are all that we are not and have made a way for us to be like you. Thank you that you give us your righteousness in exchange for our sin. We cannot do this on our own. Thank you that we don't have to, for you are with us and for us. In the name of the Father, the Son, and the Holy Spirit, Amen.

COMMISSION TO SERVE THE LORD AND HIS KINGDOM: 1 TIMOTHY 4:7–8

Have nothing to do with irreverent, silly myths. Rather train yourself for godliness; for while bodily training is of some value, godliness is of value in every way, as it holds promise for the present life and also for the life to come.

Confess to God the Father: Confess your sins to the Lord, knowing that he is faithful and just to forgive us our sins and cleanse us from all unrighteousness (1 John 1:9)

_____
_____
_____
_____
_____
_____
_____

Behold God in his Word: What does today's reading tell you about the Lord?

_____
_____
_____
_____
_____
_____
_____
_____
_____

Live for God by his Spirit: How should you respond to God's word today?

_____
_____
_____
_____
_____
_____
_____
_____

Friday | Lent III
"I Am the Door of the Sheep"

SILENCE AND STILLNESS
Take two whole minutes of complete silence and stillness to prepare your heart, soul, and mind to meet with the Lord. Be attentive to his love and care for you.

INVITATION TO MEET WITH GOD:
PSALM 84:4–5
Blessed are those who dwell in your house, ever singing your praise! Selah.
Blessed are those whose strength is in you, in whose heart are the highways to Zion.

PRAYER OF CONFESSION
Everlasting God, the thief comes only to steal and kill and destroy, but you alone give life abundantly and eternally. We confess that we have allowed thieves and robbers to steal the joy of your gospel, as we have followed after false idols that lead to death and despair. Animate and empower in us a single-minded passion for the life you offer right here and right now, that we may live out our salvation with joyful abandon for your kingdom and glory. In the name of Father, the Son, and the Holy Spirit, we pray, Amen.

SCRIPTURE READING AND REFLECTION:
JOHN 8:31–59
1. Behold Jesus: What does today's reading tell us about Jesus?
2. Live for Jesus: How should we respond to the Word today?

PRAYER OF ADORATION
Lord we need your help. You lead us into places of flourishing, but to be honest, it doesn't always look like we think. A lot of times it doesn't look we think it should. Your deliverance doesn't always look like deliverance. When we find ourselves still in the battle, still in the struggle, we ask for your nearness. And that your nearness would be our good. You will not leave us or forsake us. Remind us why that is enough. In the name of the Father, the Son, and the Holy Spirit, Amen.

Commission to Serve the Lord and his Kingdom: 1 Timothy 6:11–12

Pursue righteousness, godliness, faith, love, steadfastness, gentleness. Fight the good fight of the faith. Take hold of the eternal life to which you were called and about which you made the good confession in the presence of many witnesses.

Confess to God the Father: Confess your sins to the Lord, knowing that he is faithful and just to forgive us our sins and cleanse us from all unrighteousness (1 John 1:9)

_____
_____
_____
_____
_____
_____
_____

Behold God in his Word: What does today's reading tell you about the Lord?

_____
_____
_____
_____
_____
_____
_____
_____

Live for God by his Spirit: How should you respond to God's word today?

_____
_____
_____
_____
_____
_____
_____
_____
_____

Saturday | Lent III
"I Am the Door of the Sheep"

Silence and Stillness

Take two whole minutes of complete silence and stillness to prepare your heart, soul, and mind to meet with the Lord. Be attentive to his love and care for you.

Invitation to Meet with God:
Psalm 118:25–26

Save us, we pray, O LORD! O LORD, we pray, give us success! Blessed is he who comes in the name of the LORD! We bless you from the house of the LORD.

Prayer of Confession

Blessed Lord, you make us lie down in green pastures, you lead us beside still waters, you restore our souls. We confess that, as we walk through the valley of the shadow of death of this present age, we concentrate on all our fears, fatigue, and failures. In your goodness and mercy, lead us in paths of righteousness and rest for your name's sake, that we may dwell in your presence and peace today and all the days of our lives. In the name of Father, the Son, and the Holy Spirit, we pray, Amen.

Scripture Reading and Reflection:
John 9:1–41

1. Behold Jesus: What does today's reading tell us about Jesus?
2. Live for Jesus: How should we respond to the Word today?

Prayer of Adoration

Lord, we are your servants, and it is to be our joy to work as a servant in your kingdom. We echo Peter in saying where else would we go? Only you have the words of life. Only in you is there life to be had. Your kingship is the only one that restores our hearts and this world. Retrain our hearts and our wills to bow with joy to what and how and where you lead—to want what you want. We lay down the lesser things—and they're all lesser things—for this better-in-every-way kingdom you're building. We say together it's better. In the name of the Father, the Son, and the Holy Spirit, Amen.

Commission to Serve the Lord and his Kingdom: 2 Peter 1:5–8

> Make every effort to supplement your faith with virtue, and virtue with knowledge, and knowledge with self-control, and self-control with steadfastness, and steadfastness with godliness, and godliness with brotherly affection, and brotherly affection with love. For if these qualities are yours and are increasing, they keep you from being ineffective or unfruitful in the knowledge of our Lord Jesus Christ.

Confess to God the Father: Confess your sins to the Lord, knowing that he is faithful and just to forgive us our sins and cleanse us from all unrighteousness (1 John 1:9)

_____
_____
_____
_____
_____
_____
_____

Behold God in his Word: What does today's reading tell you about the Lord?

_____
_____
_____
_____
_____
_____
_____

Live for God by his Spirit: How should you respond to God's word today?

_____
_____
_____
_____
_____
_____
_____

Fourth Sunday of Lent

Gracious Father, whose blessed Son Jesus Christ came down from heaven to be the true bread which gives life to the world: Evermore give us this bread, that he may live in us, and we in him; who lives and reigns with you and the Holy Spirit, one God, now and for ever. Amen.

Book of Common Prayer

I AM the Good Shepherd
John 10:11

Jesus declares "I am the good shepherd" (John 10:11). Shepherds were a common feature of the ancient world, especially in Judea, where the care of sheep was essential to their way of life. Such a fundamental part of their everyday existence provided rich imagery and resonate metaphors to describe the governing responsibilities of the king (Ps. 78:70–71), the ministry of the priests and prophets (Ezekiel 34:1–10), and God's caring relationship with his people (Is. 40:11). One of the most famous lines of Scripture reads, "Yahweh is my shepherd; I lack nothing" (Ps. 23:1). Therefore, Jesus' claim of being the "good shepherd" is both an identification with the righteous reign of Yahweh and an indictment on all those in authority who have failed the people.

Jesus explains what a good shepherd looks like. The good shepherd lays down his life for the sheep (10:11). It is remarkable how Jesus flips this metaphor on its head. Usually, it is the sheep who lays down its life, offered as a sacrifice. But with Jesus, he is shepherd who offers himself as a lamb led to the slaughter on our behalf (Is. 53:7). In contrast, the hired hand, the one who works for profit and prestige, flees at the danger of wolves, for he does not know the sheep nor care for them (10:12–13). As our good shepherd, Jesus wants us to understand our relationship with him—knowing and being known—with his loving relationship with the Father (10:14–15). Just as the Father loves the Son, so are we loved.

This week, contemplate all the ways that Jesus is the Good Shepherd, who knows you, loves you, and takes care of you each and every day. Listen to his voice who lays down his life for you and let him lead you into his green pasture where you may find rest for your souls. And from this rest, joyfully participate in the Shepherd's work of bringing other sheep that are not of this fold into his one flock, so that he may be worshiped, adored, and loved.

Fourth Sunday of Lent
"I Am the Good Shepherd"

Silence and Stillness
Take two whole minutes of complete silence and stillness to prepare your heart, soul, and mind to meet with the Lord. Be attentive to his love and care for you.

Invitation to Meet with God:
Psalm 95:6–7a
Oh come, let us worship and bow down; let us kneel before the LORD, our Maker! For he is our God, and we are the people of his pasture, and the sheep of his hand.

Prayer for the Fourth Sunday of Lent
Gracious Father, whose blessed Son Jesus Christ came down from heaven to be the true bread which gives life to the world: Evermore give us this bread, that he may live in us, and we in him; who lives and reigns with you and the Holy Spirit, one God, now and for ever. Amen (BCP, 219).

Scripture Reading and Reflection:
Isaiah 52:13–53:12
1. What does today's reading tell us about the LORD?
2. How should we respond to the Word today?

Prayer of Adoration
Lord, we declare with joy that you are the Lord, the God of all flesh and all the earth. Is anything too hard for you? (Genesis 18:14; Jeremiah 32:27). We are limited, but you are limitless; but in your mercy you work all things together for your glory and our good. We are a broken people in body and in spirit. Come be our healer and mend what is torn in our world. Only you can make all the sad things come untrue, and we trust that you are doing that, Father. Be merciful to us and bring us rest. In the name of the Father, the Son, and the Holy Spirit, Amen.

Commission to Serve the Lord and his Kingdom:
Psalm 66:1–4
Shout for joy to God, all the earth; sing the glory of his name; give to him glorious praise! Say to God, "How awe-

some are your deeds! So great is your power that your enemies come cringing to you. All the earth worships you and sings praises to you; they sing praises to your name." Selah

Thank God the Father: "Give thanks always and for everything to God the Father in the name of our Lord Jesus Christ" (Eph. 5:20).

Behold God in his Word: What does today's reading tell you about the Lord?

Live for God by his Spirit: How should you respond to God's word today?

Monday | Lent IV
"I Am the Good Shepherd"

Silence and Stillness
Take two whole minutes of complete silence and stillness to prepare your heart, soul, and mind to meet with the Lord. Be attentive to his love and care for you.

Invitation to Meet with God:
Psalm 80:1, 3
Give ear, O Shepherd of Israel, you who lead Joseph like a flock. You who are enthroned upon the cherubim, shine forth. Restore us, O God; let your face shine, that we may be saved!

Prayer of Confession
God, our Good Shepherd, who lays down your life for your sheep that we may be saved from all danger, despair, and death. We confess that we have set up counterfeit messiahs, trusting in princes and chariots, who are not mighty to save like you. Gives us the wisdom and courage not to look to hired hands who work only for profit and prestige, fleeing at the danger of wolves, but to look at you, our Good Shepherd, who gives your life that we may have life in you. In the name of Father, the Son, and the Holy Spirit, we pray, Amen.

Scripture Reading and Reflection:
John 10:1–21
1. Behold Jesus: What does today's reading tell us about Jesus?
2. Live for Jesus: How should we respond to the Word today?

Prayer of Adoration
Thank you, Lord, that before any of us were, you are. You have no beginning and you have no end. And with that comes the reality that all that you are has no beginning and no end. No end to your grace. No end to your love. We will never see the end of your goodness, your holiness, your justice, Lord. We love that you are our Father and you graciously share all things with your children. In the name of the Father, the Son, and the Holy Spirit, Amen.

COMMISSION TO SERVE THE LORD AND HIS KINGDOM: ROMANS 12:1–2

I appeal to you therefore, brothers, by the mercies of God, to present your bodies as a living sacrifice, holy and acceptable to God, which is your spiritual worship. Do not be conformed to this world, but be transformed by the renewal of your mind, that by testing you may discern what is the will of God, what is good and acceptable and perfect.

Confess to God the Father: Confess your sins to the Lord, knowing that he is faithful and just to forgive us our sins and cleanse us from all unrighteousness (1 John 1:9)

Behold God in his Word: What does today's reading tell you about the Lord?

Live for God by his Spirit: How should you respond to God's word today?

Tuesday | Lent IV
"I Am the Good Shepherd"

Silence and Stillness
Take two whole minutes of complete silence and stillness to prepare your heart, soul, and mind to meet with the Lord. Be attentive to his love and care for you.

Invitation to Meet with God:
Psalm 79:13
But we your people, the sheep of your pasture, will give thanks to you forever; from generation to generation we will recount your praise.

Prayer of Confession
King of Glory, whose righteous Son who is a friend of sinners, we confess our self-righteousness by which we condemn others and our self-made standards of holiness by which we celebrate ourselves. In your compassion, expose the wickedness of our hearts and by your Spirit help us to humble ourselves and repent of our sin, so that we may enjoy the fellowship of your grace. In the name of Father, the Son, and the Holy Spirit, we pray, Amen.

Scripture Reading and Reflection:
John 10:22–42
1. Behold Jesus: What does today's reading tell us about Jesus?
2. Live for Jesus: How should we respond to the Word today?

Prayer of Adoration
Jesus you're better than all that we lay aside in your name and for the sake of your kingdom. Our treasures and dominions are a small thing compared to all that we gain from a life fully devoted to following you. So show us where we are holding on to our empires. The areas we still proclaim "mine!" Let our kingdoms fade and die their deserving deaths. Let our wills and dreams go also. Your kingdom come. Your will be done. Here. And for eternity. In the name of the Father, the Son, and the Holy Spirit, Amen.

COMMISSION TO SERVE THE LORD AND HIS KINGDOM: 1 PETER 2:9–10

> But you are a chosen race, a royal priesthood, a holy nation, a people for his own possession, that you may proclaim the excellencies of him who called you out of darkness into his marvelous light. Once you were not a people, but now you are God's people; once you had not received mercy, but now you have received mercy.

Confess to God the Father: Confess your sins to the Lord, knowing that he is faithful and just to forgive us our sins and cleanse us from all unrighteousness (1 John 1:9)

Behold God in his Word: What does today's reading tell you about the Lord?

Live for God by his Spirit: How should you respond to God's word today?

Wednesday | Lent IV
"I Am the Good Shepherd"

Silence and Stillness
Take two whole minutes of complete silence and stillness to prepare your heart, soul, and mind to meet with the Lord. Be attentive to his love and care for you.

Invitation to Meet with God:
Psalm 100:3–4
Know that the LORD, he is God! It is he who made us, and we are his; we are his people, and the sheep of his pasture. Enter his gates with thanksgiving, and his courts with praise! Give thanks to him; bless his name!

Prayer of Confession
Almighty God, who faithfully provides and protects, comforting us with your rod and your staff and making our cup overflow, we confess our persistent grumblings and our little faith. Enlarge our hearts to take in all your goodness, so that we may remember all that you have done for us and trust you even when we cannot see you. In the name of Father, the Son, and the Holy Spirit, we pray, Amen.

Scripture Reading and Reflection:
John 11:1–27
1. Behold Jesus: What does today's reading tell us about Jesus?
2. Live for Jesus: How should we respond to the Word today?

Prayer of Adoration
Jesus, we thank you that you tell us to ask you for our daily needs—that you remind us in your Word that you take care of your people according to their need. So we ask you for your sustaining mercy and provision today for us as your Body, your Church. These are deeply uncertain times, but you are the Waymaker and you are making ways for us. In our lives. In our bodies. In the air we breathe. In our homes. By the jobs you've provided to us. By the help you give us through each other. Forgive us for not seeing you, not looking for you in our daily provisions. Reorient our minds to see you in the very bread we eat. Remind us that you are a

God we can count on—because you're good and you love us. In the name of the Father, the Son, and the Holy Spirit, Amen.

Commission to Serve the Lord and his Kingdom: Jude 20–21

But you, beloved, building yourselves up in your most holy faith and praying in the Holy Spirit, keep yourselves in the love of God, waiting for the mercy of our Lord Jesus Christ that leads to eternal life.

Confess to God the Father: Confess your sins to the Lord, knowing that he is faithful and just to forgive us our sins and cleanse us from all unrighteousness (1 John 1:9)

_____
_____
_____
_____
_____
_____

Behold God in his Word: What does today's reading tell you about the Lord?

_____
_____
_____
_____
_____
_____

Live for God by his Spirit: How should you respond to God's word today?

_____
_____
_____
_____
_____
_____
_____
_____

Thursday | Lent IV
"I Am the Good Shepherd"

Silence and Stillness
Take two whole minutes of complete silence and stillness to prepare your heart, soul, and mind to meet with the Lord. Be attentive to his love and care for you.

Invitation to Meet with God:
Psalm 28:8–9
The LORD is the strength of his people; he is the saving refuge of his anointed. Oh, save your people and bless your heritage! Be their shepherd and carry them forever.

Prayer of Confession
God of Justice, who judges with perfect righteousness and faithfully reigns over all the nations as the one true Shepherd, we confess how often we neglect those who face hunger, homelessness, and hatred. In your abundant grace, align our hearts, souls, and minds to your righteous reign, that we may become a just people who contribute to your healing of the world and welcome the other sheep who are not of this fold, so that we may all be your one flock. In the name of Father, the Son, and the Holy Spirit, we pray, Amen.

Scripture Reading and Reflection:
John 11:28–57
1. Behold Jesus: What does today's reading tell us about Jesus?
2. Live for Jesus: How should we respond to the Word today?

Prayer of Adoration
Jesus, we confess we use our own nature to excuse ourselves. We think if it's who we are, we have no power over it. We glorify our bent ways in the name of self-love, and we're sorry. But you have always shown a better way. Your ways, your goodness, your kindness, your faithfulness, your gentleness over our own. You call us to better. Thank you that you care deeply for our hearts, enough to go to those places and expose our sin. Humble us to welcome your exposure. Help us to want what you want. In the name of the Father, the Son, and the Holy Spirit, Amen.

Commission to Serve the Lord and his Kingdom: Ephesians 4:3

Let all bitterness and wrath and anger and clamor and slander be put away from you, along with all malice. Be kind to one another, tenderhearted, forgiving one another, as God in Christ forgave you.

Confess to God the Father: Confess your sins to the Lord, knowing that he is faithful and just to forgive us our sins and cleanse us from all unrighteousness (1 John 1:9)

Behold God in his Word: What does today's reading tell you about the Lord?

Live for God by his Spirit: How should you respond to God's word today?

Friday | Lent IV
"I Am the Good Shepherd"

Silence and Stillness
Take two whole minutes of complete silence and stillness to prepare your heart, soul, and mind to meet with the Lord. Be attentive to his love and care for you.

Invitation to Meet with God:
Psalm 23:1–3
The LORD is my shepherd; I shall not want. He makes me lie down in green pastures. He leads me beside still waters. He restores my soul.

Prayer of Confession
Everlasting God, you are our Shepherd who sits on the throne, who guide us to springs of living water, and who will wipe away every tear from our eyes. We confess that we live as if we are unknown, unseen, unheard, straying from your goodness, truth, and beauty. In your tender compassion, help us to know that we are known, to see you see us, to hear you hear us, so that we may find our hope in you in the land of the living. In the name of Father, the Son, and the Holy Spirit, we pray, Amen.

Scripture Reading and Reflection:
John 12:1–11
1. Behold Jesus: What does today's reading tell us about Jesus?
2. Live for Jesus: How should we respond to the Word today?

Prayer of Adoration
You say in your word that if we love you we will follow your commands. You say that if we are your people we will hear your voice and obey. Build in us a reflex to be quick in our response of "Yes Jesus!" when you lead us. Help us to know your Word deeply so we can recognize your voice easily and follow it faithfully. To know you is to love you, Lord. And we desire to know you in Spirit and in Truth. In the name of the Father, the Son, and the Holy Spirit, Amen.

COMMISSION TO SERVE THE LORD AND HIS KINGDOM: 2 TIMOTHY 2:23–25

Have nothing to do with foolish, ignorant controversies; you know that they breed quarrels. And the Lord's servant must not be quarrelsome but kind to everyone, able to teach, patiently enduring evil, correcting his opponents with gentleness. God may perhaps grant them repentance leading to a knowledge of the truth.

Confess to God the Father: Confess your sins to the Lord, knowing that he is faithful and just to forgive us our sins and cleanse us from all unrighteousness (1 John 1:9)

Behold God in his Word: What does today's reading tell you about the Lord?

Live for God by his Spirit: How should you respond to God's word today?

Saturday | Lent IV
"I Am the Good Shepherd"

Silence and Stillness
Take two whole minutes of complete silence and stillness to prepare your heart, soul, and mind to meet with the Lord. Be attentive to his love and care for you.

Invitation to Meet with God:
Jeremiah 31:10
Hear the word of the LORD, O nations, and declare it in the coastlands far away; say, He who scattered Israel will gather him, and will keep him as a shepherd keeps his flock.

Prayer of Confession
Blessed Lord, you are a great God and a great King above all gods, who has made your church the people of your pasture and the sheep of your hand. We confess that we have not heard your voice but have hardened our hearts and have put you to the test, though we have tasted of your heavenly grace. In your eternal mercy, forgive us our sins and lead us into the Sabbath rest that remains for your people through Jesus Christ. In the name of Father, the Son, and the Holy Spirit, we pray, Amen.

Scripture Reading and Reflection:
John 12:12–26
1. Behold Jesus: What does today's reading tell us about Jesus?
2. Live for Jesus: How should we respond to the Word today?

Prayer of Adoration
Lord, it's a very good thing that it's your kingdom and your power. Because the empires we build and the power we throw around are deeply ineffective to hold back the horror and evil and sadness and brokenness we see firsthand. Not to mention the things that we may never see that go on in the shadows. We only need to look around to see the limits of the power and rule of men. Whether in government, or in medicine and science or in the day to day social workings all around us. We don't have control. But your power

is without a rival. Your kingdom is eternal...no beginning and no end. Nothing can stand against it. We are a vapor. You are eternal. We have a measurement. You are immeasurable. Our strength has definitive limits, but yours is utterly limitless. There is nothing you cannot do. In the name of the Father, the Son, and the Holy Spirit, Amen.

COMMISSION TO SERVE THE LORD AND HIS KINGDOM: ROMANS 12:9–13

Let love be genuine. Abhor what is evil; hold fast to what is good. Love one another with brotherly affection. Outdo one another in showing honor. Do not be slothful in zeal, be fervent in spirit, serve the Lord. Rejoice in hope, be patient in tribulation, be constant in prayer. Contribute to the needs of the saints and seek to show hospitality.

Confess to God the Father: Confess your sins to the Lord, knowing that he is faithful and just to forgive us our sins and cleanse us from all unrighteousness (1 John 1:9)

_____
_____
_____
_____
_____

Behold God in his Word: What does today's reading tell you about the Lord?

_____
_____
_____
_____
_____

Live for God by his Spirit: How should you respond to God's word today?

_____
_____
_____
_____
_____
_____

Fifth Sunday of Lent

Almighty God, you alone can bring into order the unruly wills and affections of sinners: Grant your people grace to love what you command and desire what you promise; that, among the swift and varied changes of this world, our hearts may surely there be fixed where true joys are to be found; through Jesus Christ our Lord, who lives and reigns with you and the Holy Spirit, one God, now and for ever. Amen.

Book of Common Prayer

I AM the Way, the Truth, and the Life
John 14:6

As Jesus prepares for his death he is teaching his disciples what it looks like to follow him in that death and the promise of his resurrection (Jn. 13–17). Comforting his disciples, Jesus says, "Let not your hearts be troubled. Believe in God; believe also in me" (14:1), and then sets before them the destination of this pilgrimage of faith, which is ultimately himself. "I will come again and will take you to myself, that where I am you may be also" (14:3). Thomas, along with the other disciples, has not come to grips with the reality of this destination nor even how to get there. To this Jesus replies, "I am the way, and the truth, and the life. No one comes to the Father except through me" (14:6).

All these images, whether a heavenly mansion with many rooms (14:1–3) or a green pasture with a caring shepherd (10:9–10), are used to describe the destination of faith to give us some mental handles to hold on to. But more than that, they are meant to deepen our imagination and stir our affections for the joyful engagement with God for the eternity that we are promised. So when Thomas asks bluntly where and how he can get to this place Jesus is talking about, Jesus candidly and uncompromisingly points to himself, that he is the way and the truth and the life. He is the destination and pathway. He is the aim and the means. He is the only way we get to the Father. Or to paraphrase Thomas à Kempis:

> Jesus is the way, the truth, and the life. Without the way there is no going; without the truth there is no knowing; without the life there is no living. Jesus is the way we must follow. Jesus is the truth we must believe. Jesus is the life in which we must hope.

For us, as we seek to experience the Triune God and live meaningful lives that glorify him, he graciously immerses us in the reality that Jesus is the meaning we are ever longing for, and he is the means by which we are eternally satisfied.

Fifth Sunday of Lent
"I Am the Way, the Truth, and the Life"

Silence and Stillness
Take two whole minutes of complete silence and stillness to prepare your heart, soul, and mind to meet with the Lord. Be attentive to his love and care for you.

Invitation to Meet with God:
Psalm 67:1–3
May God be gracious to us and bless us and make his face to shine upon us, that your way may be known on earth, your saving power among all nations. Let the peoples praise you, O God; let all the peoples praise you!

Prayer for the Fifth Sunday of Lent
Almighty God, you alone can bring into order the unruly wills and affections of sinners: Grant your people grace to love what you command and desire what you promise; that, among the swift and varied changes of this world, our hearts may surely there be fixed where true joys are to be found; through Jesus Christ our Lord, who lives and reigns with you and the Holy Spirit, one God, now and for ever. Amen (BCP, 219).

Scripture Reading and Reflection:
Isaiah 26:7–15
1. What does today's reading tell us about the LORD?
2. How should we respond to the Word today?

Prayer of Adoration
Give us the hearts of those who are taught, Jesus. You see what we cannot see, and you are making ways for us, God, that we cannot even begin to fathom. Align our hearts to what you're doing. Give us eyes to see how you're working, to see the things that you're healing and making new all around us already. Create in us clean hearts. Thank you for your Word, for what it reveals about you, for how it leads us to worship you in Spirit and in Truth. In the name of the Father, the Son, and the Holy Spirit, Amen.

Commission to Serve the Lord and his Kingdom: Psalm 95:1–3

Oh come, let us sing to the LORD; let us make a joyful noise to the rock of our salvation! Let us come into his presence with thanksgiving; let us make a joyful noise to him with songs of praise! For the LORD is a great God, and a great King above all gods.

Thank God the Father: "Give thanks always and for everything to God the Father in the name of our Lord Jesus Christ" (Eph. 5:20).

Behold God in his Word: What does today's reading tell you about the Lord?

Live for God by his Spirit: How should you respond to God's word today?

Monday | Lent V
"I Am the Way, the Truth, and the Life"

Silence and Stillness
Take two whole minutes of complete silence and stillness to prepare your heart, soul, and mind to meet with the Lord. Be attentive to his love and care for you.

Invitation to Meet with God:
Psalm 18:28–30
For it is you who light my lamp; the LORD my God lightens my darkness. For by you I can run against a troop, and by my God I can leap over a wall. This God—his way is perfect; the word of the LORD proves true; he is a shield for all those who take refuge in him.

Prayer of Confession
God, our Way, Truth, and Life, you are the purpose for which we live and the means by which our lives are fulfilled. We confess that we have chosen wrong paths, we have believed foolish lies, and we have rejected the abundant life you offer us. Lead us in your way, guide us in your truth, and bring us to your love, that we may become partakers in your divine nature, through Jesus Christ, our Lord. In the name of Father, the Son, and the Holy Spirit, we pray, Amen.

Scripture Reading and Reflection:
John 12:27–50
1. Behold Jesus: What does today's reading tell us about Jesus?
2. Live for Jesus: How should we respond to the Word today?

Prayer of Adoration
Sovereign in all your ways, we thank you that we can trust you. All that is before us today, you already know. All that we will encounter, and all the places we will go, you have already gone before us. We trust that you are working out a story today that is consistent with who you are and who you have always been. Forgive us for still trying to write this story to our own liking. And we thank you for gently leading us in the ways that are better. In the name of the Father, the Son, and the Holy Spirit, Amen.

COMMISSION TO SERVE THE LORD AND HIS KINGDOM: PHILIPPIANS 4:8–9

Finally, brothers, whatever is true, whatever is honorable, whatever is just, whatever is pure, whatever is lovely, whatever is commendable, if there is any excellence, if there is anything worthy of praise, think about these things. What you have learned and received and heard and seen in me—practice these things, and the God of peace will be with you.

Confess to God the Father: Confess your sins to the Lord, knowing that he is faithful and just to forgive us our sins and cleanse us from all unrighteousness (1 John 1:9)

_____
_____
_____
_____
_____
_____
_____

Behold God in his Word: What does today's reading tell you about the Lord?

_____
_____
_____
_____
_____
_____
_____

Live for God by his Spirit: How should you respond to God's word today?

_____
_____
_____
_____
_____
_____
_____
_____

Tuesday | Lent V
"I Am the Way, the Truth, and the Life"

Silence and Stillness
Take two whole minutes of complete silence and stillness to prepare your heart, soul, and mind to meet with the Lord. Be attentive to his love and care for you.

Invitation to Meet with God:
Psalm 25:4–5
Make me to know your ways, O LORD; teach me your paths. Lead me in your truth and teach me, for you are the God of my salvation; for you I wait all the day long.

Prayer of Confession
King of Glory, who makes known to us the path of life and in whose presence there is fullness of joy, we confess our lifeless devotion and our joyless worship. Have mercy on us, O God, that according to your steadfast love and your abundant mercy, that you make our heart glad, our whole being rejoice, and our flesh dwell secure, through Jesus Christ, our Lord. In the name of Father, the Son, and the Holy Spirit, we pray, Amen.

Scripture Reading and Reflection:
John 13:1–20
1. Behold Jesus: What does today's reading tell us about Jesus?
2. Live for Jesus: How should we respond to the Word today?

Prayer of Adoration
Thank you that you gently pry our hands open, taking what is not true treasure and replacing it with what is incorruptible and eternal. We confess our pride and self-sufficiency. We confess that we think we have this under control. But in your mercy you show us a better way. That our sin and twisted ways will be corrected in your holiness. The injustice, the sickness, the homelessness, the deeply sad hopelessness will be answered only in you. We cannot fix this. So come Lord Jesus, we're waiting for you. In the name of the Father, the Son, and the Holy Spirit, Amen.

Commission to Serve the Lord and his Kingdom: Hebrews 10:21–23

Since we have a great priest over the house of God, let us draw near with a true heart in full assurance of faith, with our hearts sprinkled clean from an evil conscience and our bodies washed with pure water. Let us hold fast the confession of our hope without wavering, for he who promised is faithful.

Confess to God the Father: Confess your sins to the Lord, knowing that he is faithful and just to forgive us our sins and cleanse us from all unrighteousness (1 John 1:9)

_____
_____
_____
_____
_____
_____
_____

Behold God in his Word: What does today's reading tell you about the Lord?

_____
_____
_____
_____
_____
_____
_____

Live for God by his Spirit: How should you respond to God's word today?

_____
_____
_____
_____
_____
_____
_____

Wednesday | Lent V
"I Am the Way, the Truth, and the Life"

Silence and Stillness
Take two whole minutes of complete silence and stillness to prepare your heart, soul, and mind to meet with the Lord. Be attentive to his love and care for you.

Invitation to Meet with God:
Psalm 37:3–5
Trust in the LORD, and do good; dwell in the land and befriend faithfulness. Delight yourself in the LORD, and he will give you the desires of your heart. Commit your way to the LORD; trust in him, and he will act.

Prayer of Confession
Almighty God, you are true in all that you are and faithful in all that you do, we confess that we have been false to you, to others, and to ourselves. We have not had the courage to admit all that we lack in all that you have graciously called us to be. Lead us in your truth and teach us, for you are the God of our salvation. Through Jesus Christ, our Lord, we wait for you all the day long. In the name of Father, the Son, and the Holy Spirit, we pray, Amen.

Scripture Reading and Reflection:
John 13:21–38
1. Behold Jesus: What does today's reading tell us about Jesus?
2. Live for Jesus: How should we respond to the Word today?

Prayer of Adoration
God, you are our portion. We thank you that you have said over and again that you withhold no good thing from us. We ask for contentment and confidence in the provision you are giving us now. You have said that you are all that we need, so show us what that means today. In the midst of our confusion, in our loneliness, in our fear of the future, show us how the promise you give matters: that you never leave us or forsake us, that you have given us everything that we need for life and godliness, that you are our inheritance. We

thank you that you are giving us all that we need. In the name of the Father, the Son, and the Holy Spirit, Amen.

Commission to Serve the Lord and his Kingdom: 1 Peter 1:22–23

Having purified your souls by your obedience to the truth for a sincere brotherly love, love one another earnestly from a pure heart, since you have been born again, not of perishable seed but of imperishable, through the living and abiding word of God.

Confess to God the Father: Confess your sins to the Lord, knowing that he is faithful and just to forgive us our sins and cleanse us from all unrighteousness (1 John 1:9)

_____
_____
_____
_____
_____
_____

Behold God in his Word: What does today's reading tell you about the Lord?

_____
_____
_____
_____
_____
_____

Live for God by his Spirit: How should you respond to God's word today?

_____
_____
_____
_____
_____
_____
_____
_____

Thursday | Lent V
"I Am the Way, the Truth, and the Life"

Silence and Stillness
Take two whole minutes of complete silence and stillness to prepare your heart, soul, and mind to meet with the Lord. Be attentive to his love and care for you.

Invitation to Meet with God:
Psalm 25:8–10
Good and upright is the LORD; therefore he instructs sinners in the way. He leads the humble in what is right, and teaches the humble his way. All the paths of the LORD are steadfast love and faithfulness, for those who keep his covenant and his testimonies.

Prayer of Confession
God of Life, in you we live and move and have our being. We confess that we have made for ourselves false idols, and in so doing, we have become like them—not seeing, not hearing, not knowing. May your Spirit reanimate in us the fullness of life, so that we see your glorious face, hear your gracious voice, and know your good pleasure. In the name of Father, the Son, and the Holy Spirit, we pray, Amen.

Scripture Reading and Reflection:
John 14:1–14
1. Behold Jesus: What does today's reading tell us about Jesus?
2. Live for Jesus: How should we respond to the Word today?

Prayer of Adoration
God, we have sinned and we are sorry. We rebel against you for the rightful place in our hearts to rule. Thank you for the work on the cross. Thank you for the ultimate once-and-for-all atonement for sin. Thank you for the victory over sin that the resurrection grants us. We don't deserve it. We did not earn it. But you gave it to us while we were yet deeply in sin. Thank you for your gift of salvation. In the name of the Father, the Son, and the Holy Spirit, Amen.

COMMISSION TO SERVE THE LORD AND HIS KINGDOM: 1 JOHN 3:2–3

> Beloved, we are God's children now, and what we will be has not yet appeared; but we know that when he appears we shall be like him, because we shall see him as he is. And everyone who thus hopes in him purifies himself as he is pure.

Confess to God the Father: Confess your sins to the Lord, knowing that he is faithful and just to forgive us our sins and cleanse us from all unrighteousness (1 John 1:9)

Behold God in his Word: What does today's reading tell you about the Lord?

Live for God by his Spirit: How should you respond to God's word today?

Friday | Lent V
"I Am the Way, the Truth, and the Life"

SILENCE AND STILLNESS
Take two whole minutes of complete silence and stillness to prepare your heart, soul, and mind to meet with the Lord. Be attentive to his love and care for you.

INVITATION TO MEET WITH GOD:
PSALM 77:12–14
I will ponder all your work, and meditate on your mighty deeds. Your way, O God, is holy. What god is great like our God? You are the God who works wonders; you have made known your might among the peoples.

PRAYER OF CONFESSION
Everlasting God, you are the Alpha and Omega, the beginning and the end, the first and the last of all there is. We confess that we have found our identity in that which you have created instead of you as our Creator. Since we have died and our life is hidden with Christ, help us fix are minds on the things that are above, not on things that are on earth, so that we may anticipate your glory in how we live today. In the name of Father, the Son, and the Holy Spirit, we pray, Amen.

SCRIPTURE READING AND REFLECTION:
JOHN 14:15–31
1. Behold Jesus: What does today's reading tell us about Jesus?
2. Live for Jesus: How should we respond to the Word today?

PRAYER OF ADORATION
Lord, tie us to things that breed faithfulness and obedience in our hearts. We are people who do not follow well. You lead us, but we go our own way. Tie us to the word, the Spirit, to each other. Bind us close to your side, knowing we are truly little children who need their Father to show them where to go. Thank you for being our Father. In the name of the Father, the Son, and the Holy Spirit, Amen.

COMMISSION TO SERVE THE LORD AND HIS KINGDOM: 2 TIMOTHY 2:21–22

> Therefore, if anyone cleanses himself from what is dishonorable, he will be a vessel for honorable use, set apart as holy, useful to the master of the house, ready for every good work. So flee youthful passions and pursue righteousness, faith, love, and peace, along with those who call on the Lord from a pure heart.

Confess to God the Father: Confess your sins to the Lord, knowing that he is faithful and just to forgive us our sins and cleanse us from all unrighteousness (1 John 1:9)

___

Behold God in his Word: What does today's reading tell you about the Lord?

___

Live for God by his Spirit: How should you respond to God's word today?

___

Saturday | Lent V
"I Am the Way, the Truth, and the Life"

Silence and Stillness
Take two whole minutes of complete silence and stillness to prepare your heart, soul, and mind to meet with the Lord. Be attentive to his love and care for you.

Invitation to Meet with God:
Psalm 86:10–11
Teach me your way, O LORD, that I may walk in your truth; unite my heart to fear your name. I give thanks to you, O Lord my God, with my whole heart, and I will glorify your name forever.

Prayer of Confession
Blessed Lord, we were made for you and our hearts are restless until they rest in you. We confess that we have resisted your deep and abiding rest, settling for shallow distractions, frenetic activity, and empty sedation. Awaken us to the abundant life found in your Son Jesus Christ and focus our affections on -0 truth through your Spirit, that we may find rest for our souls. In the name of Father, the Son, and the Holy Spirit, we pray, Amen.

Scripture Reading and Reflection:
John 15:1–27
1. Behold Jesus: What does today's reading tell us about Jesus?
2. Live for Jesus: How should we respond to the Word today?

Prayer of Adoration
Jesus we're not good at assigning glory to the right things. We give our praise and honor to things that don't deserve it. And we give you only our demands. But you are the ONLY one who deserves every breath we take to be poured back in praise to you—the one who made us in the first place. So we pour out our praise to the glory of your kingdom and your power, Lord. In the name of the Father, the Son, and the Holy Spirit, Amen.

COMMISSION TO SERVE THE LORD AND HIS KINGDOM: 1 JOHN 1:7

> But if we walk in the light, as he is in the light, we have fellowship with one another, and the blood of Jesus his Son cleanses us from all sin.

Confess to God the Father: Confess your sins to the Lord, knowing that he is faithful and just to forgive us our sins and cleanse us from all unrighteousness (1 John 1:9)

Behold God in his Word: What does today's reading tell you about the Lord?

Live for God by his Spirit: How should you respond to God's word today?

Palm Sunday

Almighty and everliving God, in your tender love for the human race you sent your Son our Savior Jesus Christ to take upon him our nature, and to suffer death upon the cross, giving us the example of his great humility: Mercifully grant that we may walk in the way of his suffering, and also share in his resurrection; through Jesus Christ our Lord, who lives and reigns with you and the Holy Spirit, one God, for ever and ever. Amen.

Book of Common Prayer

I AM the Vine
John 15:5

Drawing on the rich imagery of the Old Testament and what would have been such a common feature of their daily existence, Jesus uses a metaphor that would have resonated significantly with his audience: vineyards. Jesus begins by saying, "I am the true vine, and my Father is the vinedresser" (15:1). This rich, powerful metaphor has many implications for the life of the believer, specifically how one may experience the one true God.

First, Jesus is the true vine. Any hope or expectation to partake in the eternal and abundant life, must be fully dependent upon Jesus. There is no other vine. There is no other source for which we may flourish in this life and the life to come. Second, there is a mutual indwelling between the vine and the branches. Although the branches are completely dependent upon the vine, the vine produces its fruit through the branches. We are to abide in Jesus and Jesus is to abide in us (15:4), and this mutual abiding is the fullness of life itself. Third, there is an expectation that we are to bear fruit. As we abide in Jesus, as we draw from him as our vine, the source of life itself, there should be a Spirit-filled outflow of abounding good that gives glory to God. Finally, God is the source and the means of all the good we produce. Not only can the branch not bear fruit by itself, but the Divine Vinedresser actively prunes the branches to bring about more fruit. There will be pruning all throughout our life that may be painful; but we can take heart that it is always from the loving hand of the Father to participate more deeply in the Triune God and what he desires to do in us and through us.

Jesus tells us that apart from him we can do nothing. And although this text underscores the good fruit that God does through us, let us remain focused on the truth that we are called to be before we are called to do. We are to abide in Jesus, in his love, which is to say that Jesus is our home and our happiness as we experience the fullness of our gracious God.

Palm Sunday
"I Am the Vine"

Silence and Stillness
Take two whole minutes of complete silence and stillness to prepare your heart, soul, and mind to meet with the Lord. Be attentive to his love and care for you.

Invitation to Meet with God:
Psalm 31:5
Into your hand I commit my spirit; you have redeemed me, O LORD, faithful God.

Prayer for Palm Sunday
Almighty and everliving God, in your tender love for the human race you sent your Son our Savior Jesus Christ to take upon him our nature, and to suffer death upon the cross, giving us the example of his great humility: Mercifully grant that we may walk in the way of his suffering, and also share in his resurrection; through Jesus Christ our Lord, who lives and reigns with you and the Holy Spirit, one God, for ever and ever. Amen (BCP, 219).

Scripture Reading and Reflection:
Isaiah 11:1–11
1. What does today's reading tell us about the LORD?
2. How should we respond to the Word today?

Prayer of Adoration
You've told us to be peacemakers, Jesus, and we confess we often take the opposite role. Forgive us for where we have sown disunity and distrust among the Body of Christ. Forgive us for the ways we have lacked the humility and fought for our own rights and rhythms at all costs. We know that we were bought with a price, that we are not our own anymore. For we have died and our life is hidden in you. Show us how to take the low places today. To rejoice in our identity in you, and forget all the rest. In Jesus' name, Amen.

COMMISSION TO SERVE THE LORD AND HIS KINGDOM: PSALM 117:1–2

Praise the LORD, all nations! Extol him, all peoples! For great is his steadfast love toward us, and the faithfulness of the LORD endures forever. Praise the LORD!

Thank God the Father: "Give thanks always and for everything to God the Father in the name of our Lord Jesus Christ" (Eph. 5:20).

Behold God in his Word: What does today's reading tell you about the Lord?

Live for God by his Spirit: How should you respond to God's word today?

Monday | Holy Week
"I Am the Vine"

Silence and Stillness
   Take two whole minutes of complete silence and stillness to prepare your heart, soul, and mind to meet with the Lord. Be attentive to his love and care for you.

Invitation to Meet with God:
Psalm 28:7
   The LORD is my strength and my shield; in him my heart trusts, and I am helped; my heart exults, and with my song I give thanks to him.

Prayer of Confession
   God, our Vinedresser, whose Son is the true Vine and we are the branches, in your outpouring grace you bring about all existence and empower all flourishing. We confess that we so often do not recognize you as the source of our very being and we audaciously attempt to live on our own terms apart from you. Prune our souls to lead us back to you as our one true source for life that we may bear fruit that glorifies you. In the name of Father, the Son, and the Holy Spirit, we pray, Amen.

Scripture Reading and Reflection:
John 16:1–15
   1. Behold Jesus: What does today's reading tell us about Jesus?
   2. Live for Jesus: How should we respond to the Word today?

Prayer of Adoration
   Jesus, we love you. We love that you are what you are and have always been so. You are holy and we are not. We thank you that in your kindness, you made a way for us to come back to you through your son Jesus. We are not worthy to represent your name, but before the foundations of the world you chose us for yourself, to be not just your servants, but sons and daughters, coheirs with Christ. We don't deserve anything from you, and yet you gave us everything. Thank you for being our Father. In Jesus' name, Amen.

COMMISSION TO SERVE THE LORD AND HIS KINGDOM: ROMANS 8:16–17

> The Spirit himself bears witness with our spirit that we are children of God, and if children, then heirs—heirs of God and fellow heirs with Christ, provided we suffer with him in order that we may also be glorified with him.

Confess to God the Father: Confess your sins to the Lord, knowing that he is faithful and just to forgive us our sins and cleanse us from all unrighteousness (1 John 1:9)

Behold God in his Word: What does today's reading tell you about the Lord?

Live for God by his Spirit: How should you respond to God's word today?

Tuesday | Holy Week
"I Am the Vine"

Silence and Stillness
Take two whole minutes of complete silence and stillness to prepare your heart, soul, and mind to meet with the Lord. Be attentive to his love and care for you.

Invitation to Meet with God:
Psalm 62:8
Trust in him at all times, O people; pour out your heart before him; God is a refuge for us.

Prayer of Confession
King of Glory, who has so ordered your creation and your law to bring about the flourishing of your creatures, we confess that we have broken your covenant and rebelled against your righteous reign. In your unfailing commitment to our goodness and holiness, circumcise the flesh of our hearts and inscribe your law within, so that we may keep your commandments and abide in your love. In the name of Father, the Son, and the Holy Spirit, we pray, Amen.

Scripture Reading and Reflection:
John 16:16–33
1. Behold Jesus: What does today's reading tell us about Jesus?
2. Live for Jesus: How should we respond to the Word today?

Prayer of Adoration
Thank you that you gently pry our hands open, taking what is not true treasure and replacing it with what is incorruptible and eternal. We confess our pride and self-sufficiency. We confess that we think we have this under control. But in your mercy you show us a better way. That our sin and twisted ways will find their answers in your holiness. The injustice, the sickness, the homelessness, the deeply sad hopelessness will find their rest in only in you. We cannot fix this. So come Lord Jesus, we're waiting for you. In Jesus' name, Amen.

Commission to Serve the Lord and his Kingdom: Romans 12:14–17

Bless those who persecute you; bless and do not curse them. Rejoice with those who rejoice, weep with those who weep. Live in harmony with one another. Do not be haughty, but associate with the lowly. Never be wise in your own sight. Repay no one evil for evil, but give thought to do what is honorable in the sight of all.

Confess to God the Father: Confess your sins to the Lord, knowing that he is faithful and just to forgive us our sins and cleanse us from all unrighteousness (1 John 1:9)

Behold God in his Word: What does today's reading tell you about the Lord?

Live for God by his Spirit: How should you respond to God's word today?

WEDNESDAY | HOLY WEEK
"I Am the Vine"

SILENCE AND STILLNESS
Take two whole minutes of complete silence and stillness to prepare your heart, soul, and mind to meet with the Lord. Be attentive to his love and care for you.

INVITATION TO MEET WITH GOD:
PSALM 91:1–2
He who dwells in the shelter of the Most High will abide in the shadow of the Almighty. I will say to the LORD, "My refuge and my fortress, my God, in whom I trust."

PRAYER OF CONFESSION
Almighty God, you are love and in your love you have turned sinners into saints, enemies into friends, slaves into sons. We confess that we have not faithfully lived out what you have redeemed us to be. We have continued in our sin, continued in our hostility, continued in our slavery. In your unyielding and undeterred love, turn our hearts back to you, reminding of who we are and whose we are, in Christ Jesus, our Lore. In the name of Father, the Son, and the Holy Spirit, we pray, Amen.

SCRIPTURE READING AND REFLECTION:
JOHN 17:1–26
1. Behold Jesus: What does today's reading tell us about Jesus?
2. Live for Jesus: How should we respond to the Word today?

PRAYER OF ADORATION
We are your people, God. We need you to remember us as you always have. Will you give us the heart of children who know with certainty that their Father will give them what they need? You know what provision is for us. So we say yes to that. We say yes to whatever you have for us. We're not good at this, Lord. We don't trust you like we ought. Help us to see you providing and welcome it exactly how it comes. Build in us grateful, faithful hearts in response to your goodness. In Jesus' name, Amen.

COMMISSION TO SERVE THE LORD AND HIS KINGDOM: 2 TIMOTHY 3:12

Indeed, all who desire to live a godly life in Christ Jesus will be persecuted.

Confess to God the Father: Confess your sins to the Lord, knowing that he is faithful and just to forgive us our sins and cleanse us from all unrighteousness (1 John 1:9)

_____
_____
_____
_____
_____
_____
_____
_____

Behold God in his Word: What does today's reading tell you about the Lord?

_____
_____
_____
_____
_____
_____
_____
_____

Live for God by his Spirit: How should you respond to God's word today?

_____
_____
_____
_____
_____
_____
_____
_____
_____
_____

Maundy Thursday
"I Am the Vine"

Silence and Stillness
Take two whole minutes of complete silence and stillness to prepare your heart, soul, and mind to meet with the Lord. Be attentive to his love and care for you.

Invitation to Meet with God:
Psalm 90:1–2
Lord, you have been our dwelling place in all generations. Before the mountains were brought forth, or ever you had formed the earth and the world, from everlasting to everlasting you are God.

Prayer for Maundy Thursday
Almighty Father, whose most dear Son, on the night before he suffered, instituted the Sacrament of his Body and Blood: Mercifully grant that we may receive it in thankful remembrance of Jesus Christ our Savior, who in these holy mysteries gives us a pledge of eternal life; and who lives and reigns with you and the Holy Spirit, one God, for ever and ever. Amen (BCP, 220).

Scripture Reading and Reflection:
John 18:1–40
1. Behold Jesus: What does today's reading tell us about Jesus?
2. Live for Jesus: How should we respond to the Word today?

Prayer of Adoration
Father, on this day we celebrate that final feast in the upper room that signaled the sacrifice for atonement of sins once and for all. The last Passover and the first celebration of the Lord's Supper. You gathered your dearest followers around you, even knowing one would betray you, and you washed their feet as a servant. What kind of God does that? You do, Jesus. You did not consider equality with God something to be grasped or worked towards, and yet you humbled yourself here and even more so at the cross. We love you and praise you. In Jesus' name, Amen.

Commission to Serve the Lord and his Kingdom: Philippians 1:28–29

Do not be frightened in anything by your opponents. This is a clear sign to them of their destruction, but of your salvation, and that from God. For it has been granted to you that for the sake of Christ you should not only believe in him but also suffer for his sake.

Confess to God the Father: Confess your sins to the Lord, knowing that he is faithful and just to forgive us our sins and cleanse us from all unrighteousness (1 John 1:9)

Behold God in his Word: What does today's reading tell you about the Lord?

Live for God by his Spirit: How should you respond to God's word today?

Good Friday
"I Am the Vine"

Silence and Stillness
Take two whole minutes of complete silence and stillness to prepare your heart, soul, and mind to meet with the Lord. Be attentive to his love and care for you.

Invitation to Meet with God:
Psalm 43:3
Send out your light and your truth; let them lead me; let them bring me to your holy hill and to your dwelling!

Prayer for Good Friday
Almighty God, we pray you graciously to behold this your family, for whom our Lord Jesus Christ was willing to be betrayed and given into the hands of sinners, and to suffered death upon the Cross; who now lives and reigns with you and the Holy Spirit, one God, for ever and ever. Amen (BCP, 220).

Scripture Reading and Reflection:
John 19:1–30
1. Behold Jesus: What does today's reading tell us about Jesus?
2. Live for Jesus: How should we respond to the Word today?

Prayer of Adoration
While we were still weak, at exactly the right time, you died for the ungodly, Jesus (Romans 5). We are the ungodly, Father and we confess we know full well we did not and do not deserve this salvation you so freely and painfully purchased on our behalf. For the joy set before you, you endured the cross, despising its shame (Hebrews 12:2), and accomplished what you set out to do. Hallelujah! what a Savior! Thank you, Father, for sending your own son to make a way that we could become your sons and daughters. Thank you for loving us beyond our comprehension. In Jesus' name, Amen.

Commission to Serve the Lord and his Kingdom: 1 Peter 3:14–15

> But even if you should suffer for righteousness' sake, you will be blessed. Have no fear of them, nor be troubled, but in your hearts honor Christ the Lord as holy, always being prepared to make a defense to anyone who asks you for a reason for the hope that is in you; yet do it with gentleness and respect.

Confess to God the Father: Confess your sins to the Lord, knowing that he is faithful and just to forgive us our sins and cleanse us from all unrighteousness (1 John 1:9)

Behold God in his Word: What does today's reading tell you about the Lord?

Live for God by his Spirit: How should you respond to God's word today?

Holy Saturday
"I Am the Vine"

Silence and Stillness
Take two whole minutes of complete silence and stillness to prepare your heart, soul, and mind to meet with the Lord. Be attentive to his love and care for you.

Invitation to Meet with God:
Psalm 61:4
Let me dwell in your tent forever! Let me take refuge under the shelter of your wings! Selah

Prayer for Holy Saturday
O God, Creator of heaven and earth: Grant that, as the crucified body of your dear Son was laid in the tomb and rested on this holy Sabbath, so we may await with him the coming of the third day, and rise with him to newness of life; who now lives and reigns with you and the Holy Spirit, one God, for ever and ever. Amen. (BCP, 221)

Scripture Reading and Reflection:
John 19:31–42
1. Behold Jesus: What does today's reading tell us about Jesus?
2. Live for Jesus: How should we respond to the Word today?

Prayer of Adoration
Jesus, thank you that your death and resurrection dealt the fatal blow to sin and death's grip on us. You've made a way for us, as you always have, but this time it's a once and for all way to a new life, a new name, a new purpose, and a new future. We rejoice that though the shadow of death still hangs heavy on the earth, and we feel it, Lord, there is a day coming when the light of your face will dawn once and for all and every tear will be wiped away for good. In the meantime, we're so grateful that you give us rest and respite and joy even in the midst of the deeply troubling and difficult seasons. Come quickly, Lord Jesus. In Jesus' name, Amen.

COMMISSION TO SERVE THE LORD AND HIS KINGDOM: 1 PETER 4:12–13

Beloved, do not be surprised at the fiery trial when it comes upon you to test you, as though something strange were happening to you. But rejoice insofar as you share Christ's sufferings, that you may also rejoice and be glad when his glory is revealed.

Confess to God the Father: Confess your sins to the Lord, knowing that he is faithful and just to forgive us our sins and cleanse us from all unrighteousness (1 John 1:9)

Behold God in his Word: What does today's reading tell you about the Lord?

Live for God by his Spirit: How should you respond to God's word today?

Resurrection Sunday

Almighty God, who through your only-begotten Son Jesus Christ overcame death and opened to us the gate of everlasting life: Grant that we, who celebrate with joy the day of the Lord's resurrection, may be raised from the death of sin by your life-giving Spirit; through Jesus Christ our Lord, who lives and reigns with you and the Holy Spirit, one God, now and for ever. Amen.

Book of Common Prayer

I AM THE RESURRECTION AND THE LIFE
JOHN 11:25

Easter Sunday marks the greatest day the world has ever known. It is the most glorious day for the most significant day for all of humanity; the most beautiful day for all of creation the Church. To regard it as any less is to underestimate its gravity for our life today and underappreciate its glory for our life to come. The resurrection of Jesus Christ is the sunrise of our existence. Its light has broken into the prevailing darkness, illuminating the new creation that abounds before us in truth, goodness, and beauty. Easter Sunday is the culmination of the entire year, for it is the culmination for all human history—all previous days lead up to its celebration and all subsequent days flow out of it. Let us thus celebrate this day in proportion to what it actually means for our lives.

The resurrection reveals three blessed truths that should orient our heart to celebrate his grace, goodness, and glory:

First, Jesus has defeated death. Paul says that Jesus "abolished death and brought life and immortality to light through the gospel" (2 Tim. 1:10). To "abolish" death means that Jesus has defeated it, rendered it useless, taken away its power. Without the defeat of death through Jesus' resurrection, our faith would be futile and we would still be in our sins (1 Cor. 15:17–18). But because Jesus has conquered death, our faith has meaning and our sins are fully atoned, for Christ Jesus is the victorious king who has successfully ransomed all those who put their trust in him.

Second, Jesus has prepared a full resurrected life for us for eternity. Although there are people throughout Scripture who died and were "brought back to life" (i.e., Lazarus), what happens with Jesus is entirely different. Jesus' resurrection is an altogether different category. Whereas Lazarus was brought back to life only to die later on, Jesus' resurrection signifies a new body designed to flourish in the New Heavens and the New Earth. And this new resurrected body is what is in store for all those whose "citizenship is in heaven," for from it "we await a Savior, the Lord Jesus Christ, who will transform our lowly body to be like his glorious body" (Phil. 3:20–21). For this reason, Jesus' resurrection is called the "First Fruits" of the new creation (1 Cor. 15:20), for which we await our becoming fully human like Jesus Christ for all eternity. This is the hope to which we have been called.

Third, Jesus has called us live in light of the resurrection today. The essential hope of followers of Jesus is not merely "go to heaven" when we die. Undoubtedly, to be absent from the body and to be present with the Lord at death is a comfort, but it is not our ultimate goal for life. Our true aim is to participate fully in God's reconciliation of Heaven and Earth, where we may faithfully worship God in perfect fellowship in the final resurrection. What this means for us today is that all that we do here and now in this life anticipates what we will do in the life to come. After all of Paul's reflection on the significance of our resurrection with Christ he gives the Church a most practical exhortation for how we are to live today: "Therefore, my beloved brothers, be steadfast, immovable, always abounding in the work of the Lord, knowing that in the Lord your labor is not in vain" (1 Cor. 15:58). The resurrection means that all labor that is devoted to the Lord, here and now, is meaningful. As N.T. Wright explains,

> What you do in the present—by painting, preaching, singing, sewing, teaching, building hospitals, digging wells, campaigning for justice, writing poems, caring for the needy, loving your neighbor as yourself—will last into God's future. These activities are not simply ways of making the present life a little less beastly, a little more bearable, until the day when we leave it behind altogether...They are part of what we may call building for God's kingdom.[4]

In the face of death, and all our longing for God to make all things new, Jesus declares, "I am the resurrection and the life. Whoever believes in me, though he die, yet shall he live, and everyone who lives and believes in me shall never die." (John 11:25–26). The reality of the resurrection of Jesus Christ gives us hope for our future glory with the Lord just as it gives us meaning for our work unto the Lord today.

But today, as long as it is called "today," let us rejoice and celebrate and feast, for the Lord is risen.

He is risen indeed.

Resurrection Sunday
"I Am the Resurrection and the Life"

Silence and Stillness
Take two whole minutes of complete silence and stillness to prepare your heart, soul, and mind to meet with the Lord. Be attentive to his love and care for you.

Invitation to Meet with God:
Psalm 132:7–8
"Let us go to his dwelling place; let us worship at his footstool!" Arise, O LORD, and go to your resting place.

Prayer for Resurrection Sunday
Almighty God, who through your only-begotten Son Jesus Christ overcame death and opened to us the gate of everlasting life: Grant that we, who celebrate with joy the day of the Lord's resurrection, may, by your life-giving Spirit, be delivered from sin and raised from death; through Jesus Christ our Lord, who lives and reigns with you and the Holy Spirit, one God, now and for ever. Amen. (BCP, 222)

Scripture Reading and Reflection:
John 20–21
1. What does today's reading tell us about the LORD?
2. How should we respond to the Word today?

Prayer of Adoration
Almighty God, who through your only-begotten Son Jesus Christ overcame death and opened to us the gate of everlasting life: Grant that we, who celebrate with joy the day of the Lord's resurrection, may, by your life-giving Spirit, be delivered from sin and raised from death; through Jesus Christ our Lord, who lives and reigns with you and the Holy Spirit, one God, now and for ever. Amen. (BCP)

Commission to Serve the Lord and his Kingdom:
Psalm 150:1–2
Praise the LORD! Praise God in his sanctuary; praise him in his mighty heavens! Praise him for his mighty deeds; praise him according to his excellent greatness!

Thank God the Father: "Give thanks always and for everything to God the Father in the name of our Lord Jesus Christ" (Eph. 5:20).

_____
_____
_____
_____
_____
_____
_____
_____
_____
_____

Behold God in his Word: What does today's reading tell you about the Lord?

_____
_____
_____
_____
_____
_____
_____
_____
_____
_____

Live for God by his Spirit: How should you respond to God's word today?

_____
_____
_____
_____
_____
_____
_____
_____
_____
_____

On this mountain the LORD of hosts
will make for all peoples a feast of rich food,
a feast of well-aged wine,
of rich food full of marrow,
of aged wine well refined.
And he will swallow up on this mountain
the covering that is cast over all peoples,
the veil that is spread over all nations.
He will swallow up death forever;
and the Lord GOD will wipe away tears from all faces,
and the reproach of his people
he will take away from all the earth,
for the LORD has spoken.
It will be said on that day,
"Behold, this is our God;
we have waited for him,
that he might save us.
This is the LORD;
we have waited for him;
let us be glad and rejoice in his salvation."

Isaiah 25:6–9

Appendix 1:
Finding our Place in the Story of the Gospel

Stories are an essential part of who we are as humans. At the most basic level, we are constantly engaged in a wide range of stories, whether it is streaming a tv series online, immersing ourselves in an engrossing novel, or even interacting on social media. Stories, however, are more fundamental in their significance and are more formative in their substance, for they give shape to how we understand the world in which we live, and move, and have our being. It is within the framework of narrative that our beliefs, actions, and desires are given meaning, which in turn reinforces the narrative we are living out day to day. It thus makes sense that we are so drawn to stories, because life itself is an immersive drama in which we take part.

Whether we realize it or not, the world is constantly offering a variety of powerful stories that attempt to sell us a vision of the "good life" in order to form the way we believe, act, and love. For example, the narrative of consumerism tells us that the "good life" is characterized by having more and more possessions, which not only informs our understanding of happiness, but forms the way we live our lives. If we are not careful, we may be living out a story offering cheap happiness, while only giving despair.

But by his grace, God has revealed the true story of our lives through his Word that counteracts the narratives the world has to offer. In Scripture, we are presented with the metanarrative arc of Creation, Fall, Redemption, and Restoration: In the beginning, God created a good world, in which humanity, made in his image, was to represent the gracious reign of the Creator by causing the world to flourish and filling the world with his glory (Creation). Yet, the very creatures who were to represent God's gracious rule, rebelled against their Creator, wreaking havoc on themselves and on the world (Fall). Because of this rebellion, humanity's relationship with God, the world, and each other, is broken, leaving all of creation groaning for reconciliation with the Creator. But God in his rich mercy, sent his only Son to live out the story we could not, bringing reconciliation through his life, death, and resurrection (Redemption). Those who place their faith in Jesus Christ and are being formed by this story of the Gospel, faithfully proclaiming the glory of God as they wait for the Creator and Redeemer to make all things new (Restoration).

The true story of the Gospel revealed in Scripture is the "good life" offered to us. It is in this grand story in which our individual stories make sense and find their proper place; and inasmuch as we immerse ourselves in this ultimate story, we faithfully bear witness to the author and finisher of our faith. Yet, to immerse ourselves in this story does not mean to merely assent to the basic premises of Scripture (though that is essential), but to fully embody these truths in how we live our lives. We embody these truths in and through the daily habits (such as prayer, reading scripture, witnessing), weekly practices (such as the gathering as the corporate body of Christ to worship), and yearly rhythms (such as observing the seasons of Christmas and Easter). This is why as a Church we are committed to these Gospel-shaped rhythms to form us as a people who exist for God's good pleasure and the purpose of God's glory. We pray and hope that by God's grace and for his glory this guide contributes to the alignment of our hearts, souls, and minds that we may live out the story of the Gospel to the glory of Christ, our King.

Appendix II: Praying the Lord's Prayer

In the Gospel of Matthew, the disciples asked Jesus to teach them to pray. Jesus responds with what is known as the "Lord's Prayer" (Matthew 6:9–13). In many ways, it is a comprehensive prayer, spanning from the desire to see God's Kingdom fully manifest to the basic need of our daily provision of bread. For this reason, our church fathers, Augustine, Martin Luther, and John Calvin utilized this "prayer of prayers" as a guide for their prayers to God. Following this wise and humble approach, we have provided a basic framework by which you may pray through the Lord's Prayer.

The following takes each line of the Lord's Prayer and provides a particular focus along with a key passage to help guide your time in prayer. We have also provided an example prayer for each line.

Our Father who art in Heaven, Hallowed be Your Name
- Focus: Humbly and confidently address God as our Father, recognizing that this relationship is only possible through the atoning work of His Son Jesus Christ. Glorify God by revering His Name above all Names.
- Passage to Pray: Ephesians 1:3–6; John 1:9–13; Galatians 4:4–7; Romans 8:12–17; Proverbs 3:11–12; 1 John 3:1–3; Isaiah 6:1–13; Psalm 97

Thy Kingdom Come, Thy Will be Done, On Earth as it is in Heaven
- Focus: Declare your desire that God's Kingdom would come, asking that God would manifest his reign in every part of the world and every part of our soul, where we see every type of sin, injustice, and evil. Pray that by his grace God would align our will to His, that we would see the uniting of heaven and earth, and that by the power of the Spirit we would contribute to the coming of his Kingdom.
- Passages to Pray: Psalm 145:1–3; Zechariah 14:9; Psalm 93; Matthew 26:36–46; Luke 12:32–34;

Colossians 3:1–4; 2 Corinthians 5:18–20; Revelation 21:1–5a

Give us This Day our Daily Bread
- Focus: Pray that God would provide all that you need for the day, recognizing your absolute dependence upon Him for all things at all times. Pray also for God's provision of others, since we are to pray for "our" daily bread.
- Passages to Pray: Philippians 4:6–7, 19; Psalm 34; Psalm 104; 1 Peter 5:6–7; Matthew 6:26; Matthew 7:7–11; 1 Timothy 2:1; Ephesians 6:18

Forgive us our Trespasses as we Forgive those who Trespass Against Us
- Focus: Confess your sins that you have sinned against God in thought, word, and deed; for what you have done and for what you have left undone. In light of God's forgiveness granted to you because of the atoning work of Jesus Christ, offer forgiveness for those who have sinned against you.
- Passages to Pray: Psalm 51:1–4; Psalm 103:8–13; 1 John 1:5–10; Daniel 9:16–19; Colossians 3:12–13; Matthew 6:14–15; Ephesians 4:1–2, 31–32

Lead us not into Temptation but Deliver us from Evil
- Focus: Pray for God's protection in your life from evil in this world, from the evil within, and from the evil one. Also take time to pray for God's protection in the lives of others.
- Passages to Pray: 1 Corinthians 10:12–13; Psalm 20; Psalm 23; Isaiah 41:10–13; Ephesians 6:10–18; 2 Thessalonians 3:1–5; James 1:12–15

For Thine is the Kingdom, the Power, the Glory, Forever and Ever. Amen.
- Focus: Proclaim, rejoice, and take heart in the truth that the Kingdom, the Power, and the Glory belong to God. Glorify God for who He is and for what He does. With your "amen" submit all your requests to God,

trusting in His infinite wisdom that He will respond according to His glory and for our ultimate good.
- Passages to Pray: 1 Chronicles 29:10b–13; Psalm 27; Job 26:7–14; Isaiah 40:12–17; Ephesians 1:17–21; Romans 11:36; Psalm 106:48; Revelation 7:9–12

Appendix III:
The Practice of Lectio Divina

Reading Scripture is a means of grace by which we engage the Lord that forms our hearts, order our souls, and empower our strength to love God and love others. To this end, we read Scripture prayerfully that the Holy Spirit may reveal the character and purposes of God in his Word. An ancient practice for such an intentional and prayerful reading of Scripture is called Lectio Divina (Latin for "divine reading"). The practice of Lectio Divina combines several exercises that helps us to read Scripture in such a way that enables us to encounter the Living God relationally.[5] As M. Robert Mulholland Jr. explains, "Lectio [Divina] is a posture of approach and a means of encounter with a text that enables the text to become a place of transforming encounter with God."[6] The following describes the exercises of Lectio Divina, which could assist you in a deeper engagement with God in and through his Word:

Lectio Divina

1. Silence: Remain quiet in anticipation of immersing yourself into God's Word. Allow yourself time for the noise to abate and the dust of daily demands to settle in your heart to prepare a pocket of quietude in which you can meet with the Lord in this time of devotional reading.

2. Reading: Read the selected passage of Scripture slowly and carefully (maybe in two or more different translations), taking notes on the general argument and the exhortation for the reader. Look for key concepts and repeated terms without diving into too much textual analysis.

3. Meditating: Reflect upon what God is saying to you specifically in this passage. Meditate further on specific words or concepts that you found prominent. In light of this meditation, think about particular areas where the Spirit may be

encouraging you or challenging you in your walk with Christ.

4. Praying: Respond to God's Word in prayer. Specifically, use the words of the text to inform the way in which you pray. Are there certain words or phrases in this passage that can be used to pray to God? Use this time of prayer to help you receive God's Word.

5. Contemplating: Rest in God's Word, receiving what he has for you. As you have prayed and considered God's Word and what he is saying to you, actively seek God's grace to help you be transformed by the power of his Spirit for his glory and for the sake of others.

Endnotes

[1] *Worship Source Book* (Grand Rapids: Faith Alive Christian Resources, 2004), 541.

[2] D.A. Carson, *The Gospel According to John*, The Pillar New Testament Commentary (Grand Rapids; Eerdmans, 1990) 337–8; George R. Beasley-Murray, *John*, The Word Biblical Commentary (Grand Rapids; Zondervan, 1999) 126–9.

[3] Conzelmann, *TDNT* 9, 320, quoted in Carson, *The Gospel According to John*, 338.

[4] N.T. Wright, *Surprised by Hope: Rethinking Heaven, the Resurrection, and the Mission of the Church* (New York: HarperOne, 2008), 193.

[5] For a helpful overview of this practice see M. Robert Mulholland Jr., *Invitation to a Journey: A Road Map for Spiritual Formation* (Downers Grove, IL: InterVarsity Press, 2016), 129–33. See especially Mariano Magrassi, *Praying the Bible: An Introduction to Lectio Divina*, trans. E. Hagman (Collegeville, MN: Order of Saint Benedict, 1998).

[6] Mulholland Jr., *Invitation to a Journey*, 129.

ACKNOWLEDGEMENTS

It is a grace knowing that this prayer guide was borne out of communities seeking to be formed together as a praying people. We are grateful for Exchange Church (Rolesville, NC) and Vintage Church (Raleigh, NC) for the opportunity to develop this guide as the Church and for the Church for the seasons of Lent in 2020 and 2023 respectively. Many thanks to Daniel Hulsey and John Lewis at College & Clayton who graciously took on this project. Special thanks go to Daniel for his patient editing, creative design, and tireless efforts to see this guide to its end. Finally, we give the utmost thanks to the Lord who has already richly used this guide to form our hearts and shape our imaginations according to his Cross and Resurrection. We pray that he will continue to use it for his glory and for the good of his Church.

ὅτι ἐξ αὐτοῦ καὶ δι' αὐτοῦ καὶ εἰς αὐτὸν τὰ πάντα· αὐτῷ ἡ δόξα εἰς τοὺς αἰῶνας, ἀμήν.

College&Clayton Press

ATHENS, GEORGIA

https://collegeandclayton.com/books

Made in the USA
Las Vegas, NV
11 March 2025

19410055R00079